AFRICAN KINGDOMS

Lucy Mair

CLARENDON PRESS · OXFORD

1977

Oxford University Press, Walton Street, Oxford OX2 6DP

OXFORD   LONDON   GLASGOW   NEW YORK
TORONTO   MELBOURNE   WELLINGTON   CAPE TOWN
IBADAN   NAIROBI   DAR ES SALAAM   LUSAKA   ADDIS ABABA
KUALA LUMPUR   SINGAPORE   JAKARTA   HONG KONG   TOKYO
DELHI   BOMBAY   CALCUTTA   MADRAS   KARACHI

© *Oxford University Press 1977*

British Library Cataloguing in Publication Data
Mair, Lucy
  African kingdoms.
  1. Ethnology—Africa, Sub-Saharan 2. Africa,
  Sub-Saharan—Politics and government
  I. Title
  301.5'92   GN645

  ISBN 0-19-821698-X
  ISBN 0-19-874075-1 Pbk

*Printed in Great Britain by
Fletcher & Son Ltd, Norwich*

CONTENTS

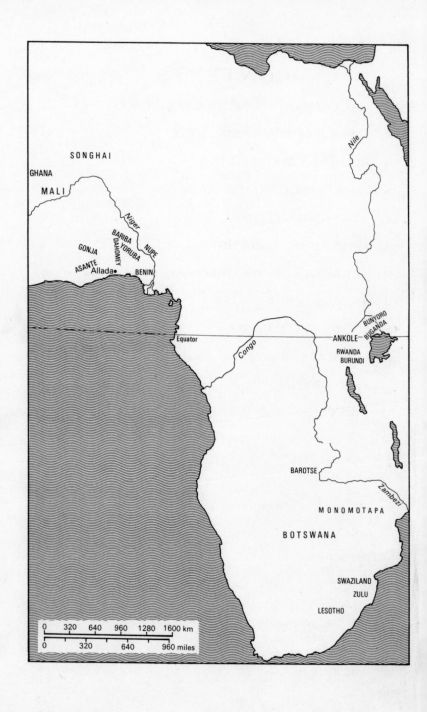

CHAPTER I

THE RISE AND FALL OF
AFRICAN KINGDOMS

IT was from Africa that we first learned how the necessary minimum 'rule of law' which makes social life possible could be secured in a quite extensive population without the recognition of any formally constituted authority. Presumably there was a time when this was the case in all human societies, and this must have lasted for many millennia. As the pre-history of Africa is reconstructed, it seems often possible to trace the imposition of chiefly authority by outsiders on 'tribes without rulers'. And the earliest historical records tell of kings who controlled the entry of strangers into their domains, mulcted them of payments in return for safe passage and permission to trade, exacted tribute from their subjects and made war on their neighbours. Most of these records come from people who visited the tropical parts of Africa for the sake of trade, and particularly in search of precious metals. Some travellers were interested also in the governance of the countries they visited, but many were concerned only with what affected themselves. From their writings we can learn at least that in most of Africa, wherever there was any valued article of trade, there were kingdoms, and that once there were kingdoms, they competed for the control of trade routes. With the great interest that has grown up, since most of Africa became independent, in tracing the history of the years before the appearance of Europeans, a surprising number of documents have been discovered. Oral traditions have been collected, and have been found much more reliable than used to be thought. Some of what is told can be checked from the findings of archaeologists; occasionally dates can be fixed by the memory of an eclipse.

Nearly every African kingdom that we know of has been described by some writer as a 'vast empire'. Both these words need qualification. If any political system established by conquest is an empire, then one could use the word of nearly all. If we mean by empire a political unit that is organized from a single centre which effectively controls its whole area, it is much more difficult to be sure how far this has been true of African kingdoms. The historian Vansina, writing of kingdoms which he would not call empires, refers to 'states, all of which had a nucleus which was tightly controlled by the central government, and all of which had outlying provinces, where the authority and power of the central government faded away more and more the further one went from the centre toward the boundary. Thus boundaries between the states were vague, sometimes even overlapping' (1966: 155–6). This is his comment on a particular group of kingdoms in central Africa, but it is of much more general application.

This book will not attempt the impossible task of making an inventory of African kingdoms. It is concerned rather to examine, from the best-documented examples, their organization and the basis of force, consensus, and ritual sanction on which this rested; what sort of reciprocity—if any—there was between rulers and subjects; how authority was divided, and whether despotism could be checked; how administration was organized; what happened to royal authority under colonial rule, and whether there is anything left of it now. The account must be set in a chronological framework, so as to give some idea what kingdoms were dominant in the major areas of Africa in different centuries, who were the rivals and which were victorious, and what areas they covered. But the examples chosen for political analysis will not necessarily be those best remembered in history; the existence of adequate data is very much a matter of the choice of field made by individual inquirers.

In so far as African history depends on the records of travellers, it falls into two sections: that which we learn from Arabs journeying across the Sahara to the savannah country on its southern fringe and that which we learn from Europeans— initially the Portuguese—approaching Africa by sea. It is to this latter section that most of the oral traditions belong. Nearly all of them lead to the calculation that the kingdoms to which they refer had their origin some time in the fifteenth century;

and nearly all of them describe their first founder as an immigrant. What this means will need to be discussed later. It would certainly not do to ascribe the foundation of 'empires' to conquerors who brought with them some ready-made recipe for 'the arts of government'. It is much more likely that modes of government were devised in the process of extending and maintaining control, and in some cases this process, or stages in it, can be traced. For whatever reason, there seems to have been a general movement of peoples in the interior in the fifteenth century comparable only to the European *Völkerwanderung* of the Middle Ages.

The Sudanese Empires

It seems possible that really effective control over wide areas was maintained in the kingdoms bordering on the Sahara, where it is relatively easy to travel, and where horses were introduced by the Arabs and could be used for quick communications and for war. From the eighth century onwards we know of empires there, the first being Ghana, which was a long way to the west and north of the present Ghana; the latter took the name as a symbol of the emergence of African independence. We know of Ghana from the writings of Muslim chroniclers and the travellers who followed the trade routes from the Mediterranean coast that were first developed in the search for gold. A Moorish invasion of Ghana, no doubt an attempt to discover where the mines were and get control of them, is recorded in the eighth century (Bovill 1968: 69). Ghana was ruled by the Soninke, one of the peoples of the region between the upper Niger and Senegal, in the interior of the present Guinea. At its greatest extent it reached from the home of the Soninke to the Niger at about the present Macina. Its capital, Kumbi, about 300 miles from Timbuktu, was said in the eleventh century to be the largest market south of the Sahara. The traveller El-Bekri described the gorgeous gold ornaments worn by the king and his attendants, and the wells of sweet water around the town. To the north Ghana was constantly harassed by Berber nomads, but at its greatest extent, when the Berbers were fighting among themselves, it took from them the control of Audoghast, the market in the south of what is now

Mauretania, to which Arab traders came for the gold that they judged to be the best in the world. When the Berbers were united under an Almoravid leader preaching holy war, they reconquered Audoghast in 1055 and sacked Kumbi in 1076. But although the empire of Ghana disintegrated after this, the Almoravids did not build one in its place to the south of the desert.

In 1203 Kumbi was again captured by the Sese, a people formerly subject to Ghana, who also dominated the Malinke chiefdoms between the upper Senegal and the upper Niger. It was a Malinke chief, Sundjata, who created the next empire, a much larger one. He began by a successful rebellion against the Sese, after which the other Malinke chiefs swore allegiance to him. Towards the end of the thirteenth century his son moved east and north and conquered Timbuktu and then Gao on the Niger, and Walata on the edge of the desert, which by that time had superseded Audoghast as the principal desert market. It was in the fourteenth century that Timbuktu, with its access to river communications, replaced Walata as the terminus of the desert trade, and it was in 1433, when it was seized by the chief of the Tuaregs, that the decline of Mali began. At its greatest it controlled both banks of the Niger as far down as Kukuya (now Bentia), while in the west the kingdoms along the Senegal and Gambia rivers as far as the sea became its vassals.

The empire which succeeded Mali was that of the Songhai, the people of Gao, who rebelled soon after the loss of Timbuktu to the Tuaregs. In 1468 the latter threw off their own overlords and offered Timbuktu to the Songhai king Sonni Ali. He in his turn extended his domain nearly to the Atlantic, covering much of the former Mali, drove the Tuareg out of Air and made vassals of the seven Habe (Hausa-speaking) kingdoms that had been established from the eleventh or twelfth century across what is now the north of Nigeria. No such extensive empire existed anywhere else in Africa before the colonial period.

The principal trade of all these empires was in gold (and later slaves); in return they acquired salt from deposits in the desert, textiles and brass pots from the Mediterranean. Arab traders were not allowed to deal direct with the producers of gold, and indeed all through these early centuries whoever controlled the mines kept their location a secret—so successfully, indeed, that it is still not certain where they were. It is thought, however, that they were probably at Bambuk and Bure near the river Faleme, where gold is still being mined by Africans; the French colonial administration did not allow foreign prospectors there.

In the period of Malian dominance only Malinke traders were allowed to buy gold for export, and a numerous trading class grew up. They came to be known everywhere as Dyula, a Malinke word for trader which has sometimes been taken for a tribal name, and many of them settled permanently at points along the trade routes, which became towns with a majority of Dyula in their population.

It was in the sixteenth century, when Songhai had succeeded to the power of Mali, that an ambitious Sherif of Fez, al-Mansur, conceived the aim of conquering the country and so gaining direct access to the gold-mines. In 1590 his army set out across the desert on this enterprise. This was the first time that firearms (some of them supplied by Elizabeth I of England) had been used in the interior of Africa, and Songhai bows and arrows gave no defence against them. The Songhai army was utterly defeated, and the Moors put a garrison in Timbuktu which they maintained until 1660. But they had no control away from the Niger valley.

To the east of them now was a congeries of small warring states, with Kanem as the furthest. Kanem has been called the first empire east of the Niger (Urvoy 1936: 321–3), though it was nowhere near the magnitude of Mali or Songhai. Its rulers spoke Kanuri, a different language from that of its Hausa neighbours to the west. The original centre of their kingdom was to the east of Lake Chad, with its capital at Njimi near the south-eastern end of the lake. Thence they extended their power northwards along the route across the Sahara, and also to the west of Lake Chad, in the country that was then, and still is, called Bornu. At the height of their first period of expansion they exacted tribute from the kingdoms of Kano and Katsina.

Royal princes were made governors of newly conquered territories, and it seems that as soon as there were no more worlds to conquer, they began to fight among themselves for the succession. While they were at odds they were constantly raided by the Bulala, their neighbours to the south-east, who eventually annexed Kanem (about 1380) and held it for more than a century. But the ruler, Omar, took refuge with a large number of followers in Bornu, and his successors gradually restored the kingdom. In the middle of the fifteenth century Kano and Katsina again paid tribute to them. Kanem itself was reconquered in the reign of the great warrior Idris Aloma (1580–1617). Under him the territory of Bornu reached an extent which was maintained until the beginning of the nineteenth century.

The last power to appear in Sudanese Africa before the colonial period arose in a curious fashion. We begin to hear of the Fulani, a people of nomad herdsmen, in the eighth century, when they pastured their cattle in the Fouta Toro mountains south of the Senegal river, among the Tekrur or Toucouleur. Early in the eleventh century the Tekrur turned them out, and from that time on there was a steady, gradual, uncoordinated movement of Fulani eastward across the savannah region. With them went marabouts—Muslim holy men—who taught and proselytized in the different cities. Gradually more and more Fulani gave up their nomadic life and settled in the towns, and in many places they eventually overturned the rulers and set up small Fulani states.

Of these movements of rebellion the last successful one was what is known as the Fulani jihad led by Othman dan Fodio, who in 1804 took control of Sokoto and thence gave his support to the subversion of the other Habe kingdoms; the new rulers accepted him as their suzerain. This latest African empire covered Northern Nigeria as far south as the line of the Niger and Benue, and for a few years it controlled Bornu; but Bornu reasserted its independence and maintained it until the time came for the country to be divided between Britain and France, the greater part being included in Nigeria.

A later holy war was launched in 1878 from the hinterland of Sierra Leone (as this part of the west coast had now become) by Samory, 'the Mahdi of West Africa'; but although his conquests reached as far as the western part of Asante, he was defeated by the French before he could establish an empire.

The Kingdoms of the Forest Area

The stimulus to political ambition in the forest area was the seaborne trade which began with the appearance of the Portuguese on the Guinea Coast in 1471, still, at that time, seeking gold; and among the means to power were the weapons which the European traders brought with them. The earliest of these southern empires was that which had come by about 1680 to be known as Asante. Its nucleus was a number of Twi-speaking migrant groups whom the British envoy to Kumase, Bowdich, writing in 1819, called 'enterprising or discontented families' (cited Wilks 1975: 110). Moving northwards from the Adanse region, they had to fight for the control of the gold-trading town of Tafo, and they combined under a leader of the Oyoko lineage which became the dynasty of the Asantehenes, as their kings were called. The first Asantehene Osei Tutu launched a number of successful campaigns, and built a new capital at Kumase a few miles from Tafo; at the same time were founded the towns which gave their names to 'the five great states' surrounding the capital, which Wilks has called 'metropolitan Asante'.

In 1701 Osei Tutu attacked and conquered Denkyira, which up to then had treated its northern neighbours as vassals, and thus opened the way to the coast and to sea-borne supplies of fire-arms. By the mid-nineteenth century his successor had extended Asante control along the coast from the Komoe (now in the Ivory Coast) to the Volta river, and had made the kings of Gonja and Dagomba in the north his tributaries. With a thousand miles of coast-line and a population of three to five million, Asante at its greatest covered an area of 125,000–200,000 square miles, and could challenge comparison with the savannah empires. But it never effectively controlled the southernmost Fante states, and in the nineteenth century the British supported them against Asante power. A series of wars were fought between Ashanti (as it was then officially called) and the British, the last in 1900. At first the British sought influence rather than direct control; they made, and tried to enforce by punitive action, agreements for the promotion of trade and missionary activity, they defended their Fante allies against the Asante, or, as the Asante would have put it, subverted their subjects, and they tried to persuade the Asantehene to give up the ritual execution of condemned criminals at his annual great festival. But when Chamberlain became colonial secretary he thought it essential to bring Asante under direct British control, and in 1896 its king surrendered without fighting to a British military force.

Further east, between the Grand-Popo and the Niger, were the rival kingdoms of Oyo, Dahomey, and Benin, whose legends give them a common origin. Such traditions have some significance in that we can see in historic times how members of a ruling dynasty, with their followers, have sometimes moved out from the original base and either attained complete autonomy or recognized different degrees of dependence on the kingdom from which they originated. As a means of expansion this was an alternative to military conquest by a centrally controlled army, and it is typical of many parts of Africa outside the region of the ancient Sudanese empires. Traditions often tell of the dispersal of the sons of an original founder after some quarrel about succession or inheritance. But what actually happened was not a once-for-all event but a repeated process.

The first significant event in the rise of Oyo that is recalled in legend is the king's refusal to pay tribute to a ruler in whose land he had settled (a story also told of Dahomey). By the fourteenth century Oyo had successfully established its independence of Nupe to the east and Borgu to the north; Borgu, with its official capital at Bussa on the Niger, enters history in its own right some time later, when it successfully resisted attack from Songhai.

The tradition of Benin is that its royal dynasty was founded by a prince given to its elders, at their request, by the ruler of Oyo. Benin was at the height of its power in the sixteenth century, when its authority extended along the coast beyond Lagos and in the north-west as far as the Ekiti area of the Yoruba. We do not know exactly when it began to decline. It lost its northernmost territories in the Fulani invasion in the early nineteenth century, while to the south those vassals who found the payment of tribute irksome could seek aid from European traders.

Oyo and the much smaller Dahomey to the south-west of it were rivals in the eighteenth century, each seeking to extend its control of the slave trade. Oyo seized territory from both Bornu and Nupe, and made tributary vassals of the Yoruba states through which the trade route ran to the coast, Egba, Egbado, and Ketu. Oyo conquered Allada, which had already been subjected to its cousin-kingdom Dahomey. At one time it demanded a share of the spoils taken in Dahomey's wars. But it never took from Dahomey the slave-trading port of Ardrah (now Porto-Novo).

The power of Oyo began to decline in the late eighteenth century, when its armies were defeated first by Borgu (1783) and then by Nupe (1791). An army leader rebelled against the king and set up an independent headquarters in Ilorin, and vassal Yoruba states began to reassert their independence. The Egba built a new capital in Abeokuta, which became the equal in importance of Oyo, and defeated the Dahomeyans after they had succeeded in rejecting Oyo's claim to tribute. Thus Oyo was already in disarray when the Fulani invasion which subdued the Hausa kingdoms reached Ilorin.

All through the nineteenth century there was fighting between different Yoruba states, a condition that the Yoruba historian Samuel Johnson calls 'civil war'. But if civil war consists in attempts by opposing armies to gain control of a unitary state, the term is not a good description of a 'war of each against all' in a vacuum of power. Many African kingdoms have been rent by civil wars between contenders for the throne, but the wars between the Yoruba city-states were analogous rather to those between Greek or Italian city-states.

With the weakening of Oyo, Dahomey became the most powerful state of the Slave Coast. Its king Ghezo refused tribute to Oyo and several times attacked Abeokuta, though never successfully. But he was able to march his troops through Ketu, from which it may be gathered that this state had become independent again; and to the west he extended his power over the hinterland of the present Togo so as to come into conflict with Asante. His son Glele dealt as an equal with British and French envoys, and died before the French decided to impose their authority by force.

The Atlantic Coast

When the first Portuguese explorer landed at the mouth of the Congo in 1482, he found himself in the kingdom of Kongo (after which the river came to be called). This had been founded in the fourteenth century, possibly by immigrants from the neighbourhood of Stanley Pool. When it confronted the Portuguese it extended about 100 miles along the coast from Cabinda southwards to the river Loje, and inland for some 200 miles; and peoples further south as far as the Cuanza—another 100 miles—would send tribute when the ruler, the *manicongo*, was able to enforce his demands upon them. Portugal regarded him as a king who was powerful enough to be treated as an ally. He for his part embraced Christianity, though not without backsliding, and his successor Affonso from 1506 sought to remodel his kingdom on Christian and Portuguese lines, and renamed his capital San Salvador. The Portuguese sent him missionaries and all kinds of craftsmen; his return was to grant them a monopoly of trade. Very early the principal item of trade came to be slaves, and not much later the Portuguese conceived the idea that the *manicongo*'s country contained vast mineral wealth, and began to press him to disclose its whereabouts and authorize them to exploit it. More and more Portuguese settled in the country, and although the official policy was to support the *manicongo* against his enemies, rivals in economic competition allied themselves with rebellious subjects. Yet the fiction of an independent ruler in alliance with the Portuguese was maintained right up to 1883. But the first Kongo kingdom was destroyed about 1570 by an invasion from the interior of the unidentified people whom contemporary writers called the 'Jaga'.

The kingdom of Angola grew up after the Portuguese presence had been established on the Atlantic coast. Around 1500 the chief of Ndongo, the southernmost vassal of the *manicongo*, gave himself the title of *ngola*, and he and his successors extended their authority southwards until it covered the area between the Dande and Cuanza rivers. In 1556 he defeated the *manicongo* in battle, and having done so, invited the Portuguese to give him the same help that they had earlier given to the latter. This time there was no question of an alliance of independent rulers. The Portuguese wanted to maintain their own security against the invaders who had destroyed the *manicongo*, and they believed that somewhere in the *ngola*'s kingdom there were fabulously rich silver-mines. They decided in 1571 to make Angola a colony and sent out the first settlers in 1574. But they could not effectively conquer Angola without African allies.

The Interior of central Africa

In the interior of central Africa the first foreign traders in the late eighteenth century came into contact with kingdoms ruled by chiefs of Lunda origin, which together covered a very wide area. This has been called the Luba-Lunda empire, and it certainly had the feature typical of an empire, that a small ruling class with a common culture imposed its authority over a great number of different peoples. But it is not so easy to be certain that the whole area was centrally controlled from a single capital; it seems more likely that outlying princes made themselves independent and refused to pass on the tribute which they collected from their subjects, and then embarked on their own conquests, as others did in the Zande state to the north of the Congo.

The germ of the 'empire' is supposed to have been the arrival around 1500 in Luba country, between the Bushimai and Luapula rivers, left-bank tributaries of the Congo, of an immigrant hero Kongolo. He and his son Kalala welded a number of chiefdoms into a single unit. Kalala's son Cibinda Ilunga, according to tradition, married a Lunda princess in the country to the west of the Luba, and *their* son is remembered as the initiator of Luba expansion.

Later generations of princes, though they called themselves Lunda, gave Luba titles to their chiefs and preserved elements of Luba ritual; the political institutions by means of which, according to Vansina, they maintained their supremacy, were Luba. The expansion of this royal lineage was going on right up to the mid-nineteenth century, when Arab slavers arrived in the country, though by that time Lunda chiefs were fighting against one another as well as against the Arabs. A recent writer maintains that the 'Jaga hordes' who destroyed the Kongo kingdom and so terrified the Portuguese were in fact the westernmost offshoot of the Lunda, who finally settled at Kasanje in northern Angola. Many different peoples in Zambia and Malawi, as well as in Zaire, say that their chiefs are of Lunda origin. The largest of the Lunda kingdoms was the latest to be formed, that of Kazembe of the Luapula. It covered the Katanga Province of today's Zaire and much of the North-Eastern Province of Zambia, and was the dominant power in central Africa for a century after 1750.

Further south was the fabled empire of Monomotapa, the ruler in whose dominions the still undiscovered King Solomon's mines were believed to lie. The story was founded on the fact that gold dust in small quantities was traded with Arabs or Swahili from the coast who penetrated up the Sabi river, and seem to have established regular markets even before the coming of the Portuguese. Monomotapa is a praise-name which has been translated 'Master Pillager'; it was bestowed on Mutota, a Kalanga chief of the Rozwi lineage, in the course of his ten-year reign of conquest. The original centre of the Rozwi kingdom was west of the Sabi river in the present Rhodesia. In the fifteenth century Mutota invaded the lands on the right bank of the Zambezi in the northernmost part of its course, where it now flows through Rhodesia and Mozambique, and moved his capital there. His son Matope extended Rozwi conquests further, until they covered the whole area bounded by the Zambesi in the north, the Munyati in the west, and the Sabi in the south, with a strip 100–200 miles broad reaching to the Indian Ocean. In modern terms Rozwi chiefs now (about 1480) ruled the whole of Mashonaland, the northern part of Rhodesia. But within a few years of Matope's death the kingdom was divided among three successors who were already fighting one another before the Portuguese appeared, and Matope's descendants held only the northern area close to the Zambezi. However, it was the son of a later invader who signed over all the minerals in his domains to the British South Africa

Company, and whose domain was held by them to cover the whole of Rhodesia.

South-Eastern Africa

The most famous kingdom in the south-east of Africa, that of the Zulu, arose only in the nineteenth century. Its expansion was chronicled by near-eye-witnesses, traders who had established themselves on the coast under the protection of the Zulu king, were treated by him rather like vassal chiefs, and sometimes went with him on his campaigns. Its earlier history was written by a missionary, A. T. Bryant, who arrived in Africa in 1883, but although he was dealing with events much more recent than those that historians are now seeking to trace in other parts of Africa, the stories he was told were just as mythical, just as much concerned with the deeds of heroes, and he accepted them without any of the scepticism of the twentieth century. What we know is that around 1800 a number of petty chiefdoms which had been roughly equivalent in power began to be dominated by one man, Dingiswayo of the Mtethwa. South African historians disagree on what prompted his conquests. Professor Monica Wilson, arguing from the history of the Ngonde kingdom in Malawi, suggests that he wanted to monopolize trade with the Portuguese; and there is no reason to rely on a single analogy for the view that that has been a common motive for expansion by conquest, in Africa as elsewhere. Leonard Thompson, however, finds no evidence of any development of trade between Dingiswayo and the Portuguese (1969: 340). Gluckman (1963) offers another hypothesis, based on the recollections of the few castaways who were stranded on the coast around the turn of the eighteenth century. He envisages an initial stage of the kind that anthropologists have observed in many places, in which lineages would divide as their numbers increased, and when a dominant lineage so divided the seceding section would take their followers with them. A population recognizing a chief from a dominant lineage was, in Gluckman's terms, a tribe, and its numbers might be anything from 'a few hundred to some thousands'. Tribes raided one another's cattle but did not seek to conquer their neighbours or drive them off their land. About 1775, however, according to Gluckman's calculation, later migrants began to find that there was no longer unlimited space for new settlement, and the more successful fighters established permanent domination over their neighbours. Of these Dingiswayo's Mtethwa confederacy, which developed into the Zulu kingdom, was the most successful of all.

If we reject the hypothesis that Dingiswayo was interested in the control of trade, this seems the only plausible alternative. But Thompson (1969: 341) reminds us that we know far too little about man–land ratios to be able to identify a critical point at which one group *must* encroach on the territory of its neighbours.

The facts of the history of Zulu expansion, however, are reasonably clear. It was initiated at the end of the eighteenth century by Dingiswayo, the chief of the Mtethwa, whose homeland was in the lower reaches of the Mfolozi and Mhlatuzi rivers, in the northern part of today's Natal, which is still called Zululand. Dingiswayo organized the manpower of his chiefdom into a standing army, and increased its numbers by taking contingents from his conquered neighbours. When he died in 1818 he was the paramount in a kind of confederacy of chiefdoms reaching southwards to the Tugela river and inland for sixty or eighty miles. The Zulu at that time were a small tribe acknowledging the paramountcy of Dingiswayo. About 1816 the latter organized the assassination of the Zulu chief who had recently succeeded, and installed Shaka, the chief's illegitimate half-brother, in his place. When Dingiswayo died a few years later (some say through Shaka's treachery) Shaka made himself paramount over the Mtethwa and all the (subordinate) allies. Then he himself extended his conquests inland, to the Buffalo river in the west and the Pongola in the north. Thompson estimates the number of his soldiers at that time at about 40,000. In his further campaigns he did not seek to subject the peoples he defeated, but to drive them away and lay their country waste in the most literal sense, seizing their cattle and burning their crops. Within a few years he had devastated the land from the Tugela to the Mzimkulu and inland as far as the Drakensberg mountains (just the area of Natal apart from Zululand). Thompson interprets this strategy, peculiar to

Shaka among African conquerors, as a means of creating a 'buffer zone' without resources, which might be hard for migrant white men to penetrate. He did not attempt to attack the populations further south who he knew would be defended by the British.

Shaka was assassinated in 1828 by a conspiracy among his kin, and was succeeded by his half-brother Dingane, who continued the policy of offensive warfare, but not always victoriously. By this time the British government at the Cape had become interested in him and his country, and the existence of a depopulated area seemed to the British in Cape Town a reason for annexation rather than a deterrent. Discontented or fearful Zulu subjects were taking refuge with white men on the coast as elsewhere they might have with rival African chiefs, and this led to clashes between Dingane and the white men. The first parties of Voortrekkers began in 1837 to cross the Drakensberg and move southwards towards the sea, travelling in wagons that could be formed into a square for defence, armed with muskets and riding on horses, those two implements of war that turned the scale in so many African battles. For a few months Dingane tried to reach some kind of accommodation with them; then he decided that the presence of any white community was a danger. His armies attacked and almost annihilated the easternmost Voortrekker encampment and razed Port Natal to the ground. But in December 1838 a new Voortrekker commando, this time bringing with them a cannon, utterly destroyed a Zulu army at the river which has ever since been known as Blood River. There were more Zulu wars after the British annexed Natal, but by that time it was the British and not the Zulu who dominated south-eastern Africa.

From about 1822 refugees from the wars of Dingiswayo and Shaka began to roam the high veld country in bands, spreading the devastation further and further, like the ripples on a pool. Historians of South Africa call them 'hordes', a word that evokes other examples of barbarian irruption into ordered communities. They plundered what and where they could, fought with one another, and the more successful gathered followers from the peoples they overran or from other wanderers.

Out of these heterogeneously composed warring bands there eventually arose two kingdoms and a conquering army which have had significance in African history; one of the kingdoms is an independent state today. These were the Ndebele under Mzilikazi, the Ngoni under Zwangendaba, and the kingdom of the southern Sotho under Moshweshwe. The last-named founded the state that is now called Lesotho from a base on a flat-topped hill in the lower Caledon valley. Here there came for refuge groups of people from many of the Sotho tribes which had been dispersed by marauders, and the amalgam came to be known as *the* Sotho (Basuto in English writings).

Mzilikazi was a Nguni subject of Shaka, who preferred to assert his independence and so be able to keep his war booty to himself, but then had to move out of reach of Shaka's vengeance. He too attracted followers by his success in war, and in ten years he increased his force of fighting men from 200 or 300 to some 5,000. By 1832 he had come to dominate the high veld, and had outposts as far away as the Limpopo, Crocodile, Vaal, and Molopo rivers, so he covered an area of about 30,000 square miles. Within this kingdom Nguni were rulers, Sotho subjects. In 1838 he crossed the Limpopo to escape the encroachments of the Voortrekkers, and built his capital at Bulawayo. Today's Matabeleland is the southern part of Rhodesia.

Zwangendaba was a subordinate chief of the Ndande, the kingdom to the north of the Mtethwa which was conquered by Shaka in 1819. He escaped north-eastwards towards Delagoa Bay, and made his way to the north, increasing the number of his forces partly by taking captives from the countries through which he passed, and partly, like Moshweshwe, by attracting other refugees who sought his protection. Barnes (1954: 13) guesses that the original seceders numbered about 1,000. They moved up the Limpopo from Delagoa Bay, entered the Shona country where they destroyed what was left of the Rozwi kingdoms, and went on, crossing the Zambezi, in 1835. Of course we do not know how often they may have paused on their journey, but it is recorded that their first halt north of the Zambezi lasted for only four years. In 1842 they reached the country of the Fipa west of Lake Rukwa, and there

Zwangendaba died. His successors separated in the manner with which we have become familiar. Two small groups went northwards, one to the east and one to the west of Lake Tanganyika. A little later two more broke off from the main body and went southwards, one to the east and the other to the west of Lake Malawi. The leadership of the main body was contested between two sons of Zwangendaba, Mpezeni, the eldest, and Mombera, who was more popular. Mpezeni's followers went south-westwards into the present Zambia, moving on until about 1856 the Bemba succeeded in resisting them. They later returned across the Luangwa river and finally settled in the neighbourhood of the present Fort Jameson, whence they sent out bands of warriors to raid the peoples around them. Mombera's, who formed the main body, settled in the present Mzimba District of Malawi, and another branch, Gomani's, in the area which is now divided between the Dedza District of Malawi and Mozambique.

Margaret Read (1956: 3–4) classified the Nyasaland Ngoni into the northern kingdom with three, and the central with four, 'separated states'. Thus we cannot speak of an Ngoni empire, or even of large Ngoni kingdoms. Their interest lies in the fact that we can trace their history in more detail than that of earlier migrants, and can see several remarkable features in it. The speed with which Ngoni bands sometimes moved on—a stay of only a few years at one base and then a long journey—is striking; it is quite different from the gradual trickle of small numbers that Vansina convincingly sees as characteristic of most African migrations. The existence of an organization that has all the essentials of a state, except the territorial base that has usually been regarded as the most essential, is again of great interest. Ngoni kingdoms, small as they are, must figure in any discussion of modes of organization. It is also worth noting that the unidentified 'Jaga' who attacked the Portuguese and their African allies of the Kongo kingdom were described in contemporary accounts in terms that might well fit the Ngoni. Vansina (1966: 57) draws the comparison: 'They lived permanently on a war footing in fortified camps. They would kill their babies [not recorded of Ngoni] so as not to be hindered by them in their march, but they adopted youngsters of both sexes from the areas they overran and incorporated them into their camps. Vast numbers of people could thus be aggregated quite quickly.' He quotes from Andrew Battell, the English sailor who lived for two years in a Jaga band, the statement that out of 16,000 people in the camp only fourteen or fifteen were Jaga by origin. Jaga kingdoms—if we can so call them—were dispersed, like those of the Ngoni, not, as in so many cases, contiguous with their parent states.

Between the Great Lakes

The interior of East Africa was not visited by literate travellers until the nineteenth century, and if there were early empires there, their existence can be known only by asking whether archaeological remains give support to oral traditions of the distant past. Such traditions tell of a great kingdom of Kitara, ruled by a dynasty of light-skinned supermen, the Cwezi; they do not agree as to exactly where it was. The name is claimed today by the people of Bunyoro, which is now a single administrative district of Uganda. Bunyoro was the dominant power in the Interlacustrine region in the early nineteenth century, but not all writers agree that it was the centre of the earlier Kitara. In Mubende district, the southern part of Bunyoro, which was included in Buganda under British administration, there is a line of great earthworks which has always been associated with the Cwezi; whoever organized their construction was in a position to mobilize considerable manpower. Radiocarbon tests ascribe the earthworks to the period 1350–1500. The historian Roland Oliver interprets them as a defence against invasion from the north, and concludes that the centre of Kitara was in Ankole, south of Bunyoro, that its effective power was in the south, and that the Cwezi ruled Bunyoro for only about fifty years.

Ankole tradition makes them masters of the present Bunyoro, Toro, Ankole, Karagwe (in Tanzania), and at least the northern part of Rwanda. But Rwanda has no tradition of subjection to Kitara. The Nyoro say that after only two reigns the Cwezi miraculously disappeared; Oliver considers that this story masks their defeat in war and retreat to the south from their northern outpost.

There is no doubt that their successors, the Bito, based their 'empire' on Bunyoro. Speke, in the map which he published in 1862, shows Bunyoro as 'the ancient kingdom of Kitara'. 'At its zenith', says Beattie (1971: 28), 'it is said to have extended over most of present-day Uganda, and beyond it into Tanzania, the Congo and the Sudan.' To the north of Bunyoro, the Acoli and Alur have traditions that their chiefs had to be confirmed in office by the king of Bunyoro, and the Alur also claimed the Bito kings as their kinsmen. One could take such statements as evidence of effective suzerainty of the kind exercised by the Sultan of Sokoto over the other Fulani emirs in Nigeria, or of a ritual supremacy of the kind exercised by Oyo over the Yoruba states, or of an outward dispersion of members of a ruling class of the kind described among the Lunda.

This last interpretation seems the most probable, since the traditions say that Rukidi, the first Bito king of Bunyoro, appointed his kinsmen to rule provinces, and that they or their descendants threw off his authority and made themselves independent. In the reign of Rukidi himself, the story goes, his twin brother whom he had made governor of Buganda repudiated his allegiance. (The Ganda reject this version of 'history' and say that their royal dynasty was much older than the Bito.) Later Busoga (east of Buganda), Ankole and Karagwe seceded in the same way (and also Rwanda if it ever had a Bito chief). Many wars were fought against Buganda and some against Ankole.

At the time of Speke's visit (1862) the King of Bunyoro was suzerain over a great part of Buganda, much of Toro and Ankole, and of Karagwe to the south of them. As late as 1892 Gessi Pasha referred to a powerful Acoli chief in the north who 'gave to Kaba Rega all the ivory he collected'. It is possible that the balance had begun to tilt in favour of Buganda when that country was acquiring guns through trade with the Arabs, but the ultimate supremacy of Buganda was a matter of its alliance with Britain.

To the south of Ankole lies Rwanda, a kingdom the history of which has been microscopically studied by Belgian scholars through its rich corpus of traditions. The reconstructed history of Rwanda is of extreme interest for the understanding of processes of state-building, but the kingdom as such was never an African great power.

This brief survey is intended to provide a few fixed points in time and space for readers who may be new to the vastness and variety of the African continent and its societies. It mentions a number of kingdoms that will not be discussed again, and does not mention some that will be considered in detail. The reason is that an anthropologist's choice of an area for study does not necessarily lead him to a people who have played a great part in recorded history or to rulers whose ancestors have conquered empires. The Azande, the Lozi, the Swazi, to give some examples, have been admirably documented by anthropologists who combined an interest in the past with the techniques of participant observation, but they do not occupy many of the pages in histories of Africa. It is to the peoples whose political structure has been thoroughly studied, so that the outlines which are all that tradition gives us are filled in from direct acquaintance with what is left today of royal people, that we must look in seeking to identify the characteristics of African kingdoms.

CHAPTER II
THE BUILDING UP OF KINGDOMS

ONE theory of the rise of African kingdoms is that the notion of kingship somehow spread from a single source in Egypt. It appears from archaeological evidence that the technique of iron-working originated in Meroe on the Nile and was gradually diffused throughout the continent. But it is hard to picture kingship as a technique which somebody has brought with him to practise in a new place. The argument rests largely on similarities in the ritual of kingship in widely separated places; it presupposes behind these rituals an idea of 'divine kingship' the precise nature of which is taken for granted. All peoples surround royal office with ritual, and we can find instances far from Africa in which miraculous powers are attributed to kings. The word 'divine' seems to have been taken over from *The Golden Bough* without much thought about what corresponds to it in the view of the peoples who are alleged to view their kings as divine. Modern structuralists might well ascribe the similarities in royal rituals to those unconscious mental structures that constrain all human thought. If one is concerned with the secular aspects of kingship, which rituals or ideas about divinity cannot replace but at best underpin, one has to envisage gradual processes of securing and consolidating power. Of course there is a stage, as kingdoms grow into empires, when the latest conquest is fitted into an existing system, but this is not and cannot be how kingships originated. What we want to know is how individuals were able to make themselves kings, how they manoeuvred and improvised in order to maintain and improve their positions; the later stages can sometimes be followed from recorded history.

In every African kingdom a tradition is preserved of the origin of the ruling dynasty. This tradition asserts the claim of a single descent line to sole right to rule, and in that respect is what Malinowski called a 'mythical charter', an account of the past that serves to justify the present. Sometimes, as in the case of the Chwezi stories, the original rulers are indeed endowed with miraculous powers. Sometimes such first kings are supposed to have brought 'civilization' to people who were living like animals, hunting for their food, knowing nothing of cattle, fire or any of the useful arts. An example is the Rwanda myth of Kigwa, who fell from heaven and in that sense could be considered divine (Vansina 1962: 43). The Nyakyusa story of the coming of Lwembe, the hero-ancestor of their kings and chiefs says, in one version, that at his arrival they were already cultivators, but, knowing no fire, they are their food raw. Lwembe also brought them iron, which of course would have been no use to a people without fire (Wilson 1959: 3, 13). But for the majority of the Nyakyusa, the heroes brought grain food with them too.

These stories reflect the tellers' idea that it is 'uncivilized' to be without a ruler. Others conceal a break in dynastic continuity by forging, we might say, a link of indirect kinship between the displaced lineage and its successors. Where the political function of a tradition is so obvious there is reason to suspect its factual truth.

But there are other traditions that are so to speak neutral. There is not much political capital to be made by claiming descent from an immigrant without claiming extraordinary powers for him; yet a number of traditions lead back to a man who headed an immigrant group, and after becoming dissatisfied with a situation of dependence, rebelled and seized political power. It is after this initial act that the period of conquests, often attested by evidence from other sources, begins.

It is clear that there must have been a time when there were no kingdoms in Africa, or indeed anywhere in the world. In the beginning all men were hunters, moving about in small bands. When they learned to domesticate plants and animals they formed larger autonomous groups within populations recognizing in common the elementary norms of respect for life and property. Among nomad pastoralists such groups are usually based on patrilineal descent; settled cultivators too may be organized in this way. All these different types of society still exist for our observation, but what is harder to see is the slow process by which one lineage establishes domination over the rest and comes to be regarded as the one with unquestioned right to fill the office of chief or king. Indeed it had already become impossible to follow such a process by the time that anthropologists had realized the importance of close first-hand observation, since European rule everywhere either destroyed or distorted the political systems of independent Africa. In the corpus of African ethnography there are only one or two examples which may bear on this question.

One of these is Philip Mayer's (1949) study of the Gusii in western Kenya, a people divided into seven tribes, and these again into clans, each of them autonomous in its own territory. In every tribe except one, there was a lineage of 'owners of the land' and others attached to it by affinal or matrilateral ties, but there was no significant difference of status between them, and all were regarded as ultimately akin. The seventh tribe consisted of the people of Getutu. For whatever reason, Getutu was a place of refuge for people driven from their homes by raiding Masai or Kipsigis, the pastoral neighbours of the Gusii. These exiles would attach themselves to individuals who would give them protection and cattle to marry with; accordingly they were called 'bought people', and sometimes one would repay the cattle and go home. But those who stayed, and their descendants, were never 'adopted' as were immigrants to the other six tribes; they were political subjects of the 'owning' lineage, Nyakundi. Whereas among the other six tribes claims for debts or compensation were matters to be dealt with by the lineage representatives of the parties, in Getutu the different Nyakundi lineages acted on behalf of their 'bought people' in such disputes, and elders of one Nyakundi lineage would be recognized throughout the tribe.

This does not get us very far, particularly as Nyakundi, though in a sense jointly rulers, were not a minority but over half the population of Getutu, with their dependants a fringe of miscellaneous immigrants. What is perhaps more significant in the light of what we have learned about the origin of some kingdoms is a negative point: the apprehension of all Gusii that a lineage of strangers might oust the rightful owners of the land. 'If a sister's child is buried at our place', they say, 'his house will become many and ours will die out' (Mayer 1949: 28). In other words, be careful not to let him forget his stranger origin. The proverb may well spring from fear rather than experience; but when one reflects that the immigrant lineages of the historical traditions must have intermarried with their hosts—they could not otherwise have lived with them in amity—one can only comment that, as they say, 'There's something in it'.

Evans-Pritchard (1940: 185–9) offers another conjecture as to the process by which a central authority might be created in a population divided into autonomous and often mutually hostile segments. In the southern Sudan at the time of the Mahdist revolt against Egyptian rule, which was also a movement of Arab aggression against the Nilotic peoples, prophets arose among the Nuer who called on them to unite against their external enemies. The prophet who gained the most widespread influence, Ngundeng, appeared later, in 1906, as an opponent of British authority. He had been a 'leopard-skin chief', to use the name applied to such ritual experts by British administrators, or an 'earth-priest' as Evans-Pritchard came to call them later. Thus he belonged to a lineage believed to have the monopoly of a certain kind of ritual power. His fame spread all through the eastern half of Nuer country, and a great pyramid, made of ashes and other debris from cattle camps, some sixty feet high and surrounded by a ring of ivory tusks, was built by his followers in his honour and that of the sky-god by whom he was supposed to be possessed. If this was an organized enterprise, we must assume that Ngundeng had acquired considerable powers of command. If, on the other hand, the pyramid was just added to by the individual contributions of people who came to pay their respects to the prophet, as, on a smaller scale, passers-by add pebbles to a cairn, it is not evidence of effective political authority. There is no doubt that Ngundeng's fame spread far and wide, but when we ask what forces he could muster for the rebellion that he preached, the answer is that the largest on record consisted of 300 men.

But the belief that ritual powers are hereditary, and so are the monopoly of particular lineages, is much older than kingship. Should we then expect the founders of kingdoms to have been ritual experts, or members of such specially endowed lineages? The myths rarely ascribe any such status to them, although the Nyakyusa Lwembe is said to have possessed the special medicines of chiefship. But kingdoms once founded are sometimes able to extend their rule over kingless peoples because the latter believe the ritual power of kingship to be something that they cannot generate from among themselves. Yet the first example that I have to offer does not illustrate such a situation.

The Rise of Rwanda

The richest oral tradition to have been examined by a historian is that of Rwanda, and the most detailed exercise in disentangling history from myth is the work that has been done on this corpus of records (committed to writing in recent years) by Jan Vansina (1962). He has reconstructed a picture of the country that is now Rwanda, as it seems likely to have been at the time when Nilotic herdsmen of the people who later became known as the Tutsi began to enter it. At that time the Hutu cultivators were organized partly in tribes of autonomous lineages and partly in tiny chiefdoms with hereditary rulers, a description that parallels what a contemporary anthropologist, Aidan Southall, observed among the Alur and their neighbours on the Nile–Congo divide just north of Rwanda. Where the Hutu recognized chiefs, the latter were held to have ritual powers; they controlled the weather, causing rain to fall at the right time and not in excessive quantities, and they combated disasters such as locust invasion. Such powers were ascribed to the Alur chiefs too, and the neighbouring acephalous peoples, believing that they were an inseparable element in the quality of chiefliness, sought the sons of Alur chiefs to rule over them rather than looking to leaders among themselves.

Again we cannot learn how a special ritual power came to be claimed in the first place: Vansina simply says that the heads of certain lineages came to be regarded as chiefs. They had little secular authority, and they could not prevent the waging of blood-feuds among their subjects. These chiefdoms had certain ritual features that later characterized the kingdom of Rwanda; the sacred symbol of rule was a drum, and the priests who were responsible for royal burials were called *abiru*, a name that was taken for similar people in the embryonic Tutsi kingdoms, and later for Rwanda.

Into this country came the immigrant herdsmen from the north. Some of them made no attempt to dominate particular areas, but moved to and fro with their cattle as their descendants do to this day. But the others became the pastoral ruling class that was maintained in authority first by the Germans and then by the Belgians. As Vansina reconstructs the picture, bands of herdsmen arrived together, recognizing one man's leadership in the choice of route and of pastures. In matters of internal authority the heads of descent-groups and their successors remained largely independent, and it would seem that each group kept to its own grazing lands, since otherwise there could have been no analogy between lineage heads and territorial chiefs. There early existed some kind of patronage system whereby men with favours to offer, notably gifts or loans of cattle, could gather a following of dependants who would serve them and support them in a fight. The one who came to be a king must have been the most successful of these. In the central area, the nucleus of today's Rwanda, the herdsmen settled cheek by jowl with Hutu populations, and seem to have achieved domination over them by offering individual protection and the use of cattle in return for labour or tribute in grain or beer—the *ubuhake* relationship for which Rwanda is famous. Vansina states definitely that in these early days there was little ritual attached to kingship.

At the time when the curtain rises on Rwanda's story, such kings had begun to appoint their own brothers and sons as rulers over divisions of the country in the place of lineage heads. This policy strengthened a royal lineage in relation to the rest, but it opened the way to secession for those who were far enough from the centre of power, and had enough followers of their own, to make themselves independent. Thus the germ of the historical Rwanda was a chiefdom of Bugesera, a kingdom founded by secession from Gisaka, itself a seceder from Mubari, which the traditions say was the first kingdom to be founded.

All these places were on the eastern and south-eastern borders of the present Rwanda.

Two brothers, Mukobanya and Mutabazi, in the early sixteenth century, finally detached Rwanda from Bugesera and set about extending its power over neighbouring petty Tutsi kingdoms. They conquered Bumbogo and Rukoma, where the ruling lineages claimed ritual powers similar to those described as belonging to Hutu chiefs, and called themselves *abiru*. Mukobanya attached these lineages to his court, as guardians of the royal insignia and priests who carried out rituals in secret, the mystery of which enhanced the prestige both of the king and of the *abiru* themselves. Vansina asserts that the notion of the ritual responsibility of the king for the welfare of the country arose only after the incorporation of the *abiru*. They exercised secular as well as ritual power, since they continued to control their former kingdoms, now as fiefs from the king. Later kings created new *abiru* to reward favoured subjects, making them keepers of newly devised ritual objects, or in some other way giving each his special function along with their combined duty of preserving the ritual secrets and having the rites performed when it was time for them. The association of the individual person of the king with the welfare of the whole country came eventually to create an ideology of national unity which, though it could not prevent wars between contenders for the throne, did discourage ideas of secession among Tutsi.

But secular power cannot rest on ritual alone. Indeed it is not made effective at all without the delegation of authority to secular officials in charge of divisions of the kingdom; this is a necessary limitation on central power, and kings who wish to remain paramount must somehow counteract it. As long as territorial authorities recruit their own armies, rebellion is too easy; what the Rwanda kings tried to do—mainly, of course, in the interests of military efficiency—was to centralize the army.

The earliest fighting forces were bands attached to any man who could attract a following by his success in raiding cattle. Mutabazi was able to forbid the recruiting of warriors by chiefs who had not his permission. He and his successors soon after they came to the throne called on leading Tutsi to send their sons to court, where they were trained in the use of weapons and in the bearing appropriate to an aristocrat. About 200 young men were recruited at a time, and in a long reign new bands were formed at intervals. But these were a royal body-guard rather than a national army; they must often have had to fight for the king against his over-mighty subjects.

The centralization of all fighting forces seems to have begun in the late eighteenth century. According to a recent inter-pretation of some lineage traditions (Rwamukumba and Mudandagizi 1974) this was the time when the Tutsi began to clear the forests and claim hereditary rights to the pastures that they had created, instead of roaming at large through the country. By this time the king was strong enough to assert his authority to appoint the chiefs of new armies, though once appointed they expected to pass on the office to their sons. The king assigned to each army its pastures on the frontiers of the country, and required the warriors to live in camps at strategic points; this may have been a means of controlling recently conquered populations as well as of defence. The army chief was now made the authority over all the inhabitants of his area, not only the warriors.

The king himself had no army, and therefore had to find other means of securing his supremacy. Both to protect them-selves against the army chiefs and to consolidate Rwanda's hold over conquered territories, later kings built subsidiary capitals in different parts of the country, in each of which they would establish a queen and a retinue, with an official to see to the provisioning of the capital from the resources of the country around it. Eventually the whole of Rwanda came to be divided into districts—much smaller areas than the regimental provin-ces—under civilian chiefs who had no armies at their disposal. Only then, says Vansina (1962: 71), could the king really be called supreme. A yet further development was the division of district authorities into 'land chiefs' and 'cattle chiefs' respons-ible for tribute in grain and beer, and cattle, respectively. Rivalry between these paired officials for royal favour made them jealous keepers of each other's conscience, always ready to detect and report misdemeanours and quite unable to com-bine against superior authority.

Rwabugiri, who reigned from 1860 to 1895, had made himself powerful enough to disregard lineage claims to hereditary office, even those of divisions of the royal clan, and appoint his own creatures to all positions of authority. He freely dismissed chiefs from office and had them put to death, and even disregarded and humiliated the *abiru*. He himself was eventually assassinated, but his successors followed his example, and both German and Belgian administrations supported this version of royal power.

Such highly centralized control, however, was fully effective only in the oldest parts of the kingdom, where there was the largest Tutsi population and the Hutu had accepted Tutsi rule for centuries. In the areas conquered in the late eighteenth and nineteenth centuries the position was different. There, although no rival ruler was tolerated, both the nature and the effectiveness of administrative arrangements varied widely from one region to another. In some places an army chief was in charge of the collection of tribute from newly acquired subjects, in others a trusted local Hutu chief; occasionally such an official might be one of those Tutsi who, in the outlying areas, had lived side by side with the Hutu but not intermingled with them as in the centre of the kingdom.

The effectiveness of control depended very largely on the proportion of Tutsi in a given district, whether these were new colonizers or had been there before the Rwanda conquest. In many cases Hutu refused to pay tribute, and punitive expeditions were sent against them. This might be followed by the gradual substitution of the king's men for local chiefs at all levels of authority. Many of the revolts in the history of Rwanda, including some in the present century, were led by the representatives of lineages thus displaced. But until the final bloodbaths of 1959 and later years, we do not learn of rebellions against Tutsi domination in the central region where the *ubuhake* system of clientship—some call it serfdom—was most firmly established.

It is only from Rwanda that we hear of a deliberately created ritual relation between descent groups and the king. Writers on other Interlacustrine kingdoms (e.g. Fallers 1964) take this as something that has 'always' existed, and it is doubtless futile to ask whether a conqueror rewarded his followers with ritual offices as soon as his position was assured, or whether they were created in some other circumstances. In both the Ganda and Nyoro states certain clans had the right and duty of providing keepers of different objects of the royal regalia, of performing certain parts of the installation and later 'refresher' rituals of the king, and of undertaking the secular responsibility of supplying the palace with essential foodstuffs and objects of craftsmanship such as pots. In Buganda the senior of these were chiefs controlling large areas of land (*masaza* or counties), and up to the time of British overrule the three most important of these offices were effectively claimed by heads of clans. The rest came more and more to depend on the king's pleasure, but in the case of the three major chiefs the assertion of the king's supremacy had to be made in a roundabout manner, by controlling the appointment of their subordinates. It was also possible to weaken the power of a clan head or any other chief without actually demoting or dismissing him, by carving out sections of his domain and allocating them to a queen or prince, or a favoured warrior or palace servant.

Buganda developed a national army only late in the nineteenth century. When guns were introduced into the country by Arab traders, Mutesa I created a new chiefship with the title Mujasi, which is derived from the Swahili word for 'brave'. Mujasi was responsible for the guns kept at the palace; he had scattered estates all over the country, unlike other chiefs, each of whom controlled a single block of land, large or small, and in each of these he raised a band of men who had already proved to be good fighters, and who were now available when summoned, unlike the earlier warriors who were recruited ad hoc by their territorial chiefs (Southwold n.d. [1961]: 14). But Mutesa did not attempt to control the acquisition of guns by other chiefs. His successor Mwanga created a palace bodyguard from young men who already had guns; some had received these from local chiefs and then left their service. This measure reduced the power of the chiefs versus the king, but it turned against him when the soldiers rebelled and the territorial chiefs were unable or unwilling to come to his aid.

The Story of Dahomey

The legends of a hero who marries a king's daughter and begets the founder of the current dynasty are certainly intended to legitimize the descendants of someone who may have been a usurper. It is not very likely that the fabled hero arrived alone in his new country. Vansina's reconstruction of the Rwanda story gives us the picture of a number of descent groups migrating into sparsely populated land or displacing the inhabitants, but not at first imposing themselves as rulers. The west African counterpart to Rwanda is Dahomey, in the sense that there too there were guardians of the royal traditions, whose duty it was to preserve them by memorizing them, and to recite them on prescribed occasions. Unlike the *abiru*, these bards were descendants of the kings whose reigns they celebrated.

In the Dahomeyan tradition it is a leopard and not a hero who marries the princess and founds a new dynasty, the Agassuvi. The actual story as it is envisaged by Newbury is what must have been typical of many of the later-founded African kingdoms. The migrants from Allada, the original home, were 'roving bands of raiders under war-chiefs who acquired land rights by the generosity of their neighbours or by force' (Newbury 1961: 10). One of these war-chiefs 'staked out a *de facto* claim to paramountcy by his qualities of leadership in the struggle of the Agassuvi for new land and water rights'; on this interpretation he had no hereditary claim at that stage. The immigrants ingratiated themselves with their hosts by making them presents, but as more and more people from Allada followed them, the local chief began to be concerned about their power, and eventually he sent his messengers to root up their crops. At this they rebelled and killed him, no doubt with the support of those of his subjects whom they had won over. Argyle (1966: 8) injects a sense of proportion into the story by reminding us that at the death of Dako, the rebel leader's successor, the Agassuvi 'were in possession of an area of about five miles' radius from the point where they had first settled'. These small conquests took them about twenty-five years.

Dako's successor, Wegbadja, collected a tax from his subjects to buy guns from the coast, and he is said to have abolished the right of private vengeance for homicide and required all capital cases to be brought to him. This last is everywhere a criterion of effective central rule, though sometimes, as in Buganda, the royal power is asserted merely by the requirement that persons seeking vengeance must have royal authorization. We do not often find the insistence on the royal monopoly of capital punishment ascribed to a particular ruler. It is of course a part of the assertion of the primacy of royal power over lineage autonomy.

The Dahomeyan kings had to be wary, like all hereditary rulers, of competition from their own kin. Tradition holds that at no time was any member of the royal clan appointed to a position of authority; thus an unusually large number of people were excluded, and Dahomey appears as the polar opposite of the south-eastern Bantu kingdoms in which all territorial offices were held by royals. At the same time, the commoner officials in Dahomey never established a claim to pass on their office to their sons.

In this respect Dahomey contrasted sharply with the southern cousin-kingdoms of Allada and Whydah, where the Agassuvi left a considerable measure of autonomy to the autochthonous lineages among whom they settled. The twenty-six provinces of Whydah—none a very large area—were subject to hereditary governors, doubtless the heads of such lineages, who were able independently to collect tolls on trade caravans passing through their land. As the state of affairs was seen by an eighteenth-century traveller (Labat, 1730: 98), the immigrant kings were still regarded as intruders to such an extent that they were afraid to confront any of the lineage heads for fear of provoking a general rebellion.

Another contrast was in military organization. Although there does not seem to have been a standing army comparable with those of the Zulu and of Rwanda, the fighting force of Dahomey did not consist, as it did in Allada, and until a quite late date in Buganda, simply of bands led by their territorial chiefs. It was recruited territorially, but the soldiers were then allotted to a right and left wing which were not territorially based. The commanders of the right and left wings were the two chief ministers, whose office was hereditary.

Some Other Kingdoms

The founding of the Basuto nation is a matter of historical record; it grew up by the accretion of tribes or sections of tribes, or fleeing individuals, displaced from their homes by the devastations of Shaka, in the period of ten years from 1822. But the events that are recounted—raiding for cattle, migrations, the making and breaking of alliances, offers and repudiations of allegiance—are just what must have been typical of the anarchic conditions in which earlier kingdoms were created. According to the old men whose memories were recorded by the missionary Ellenberger, Moshweshwe had had from his youth the ambition to be a great chief; but although he early demonstrated his prowess in successful raids, it was by offering protection to those who sought it that he built up his power. At first these refugees were victims of the roaming hordes who, driven out by Shaka, drove others before them. Later there were added to these Africans turned off their land by migrant Boers. Geography helped Moshweshwe; after moving once or twice with a few thousand followers, he settled on a flat-topped mesa, Thaba Bosiu, that was almost inaccessible. He knew when to make alliances with other chiefs of small groups and when to buy off powerful enemies by paying tribute. As the number of his subjects increased, he had to be able to distribute the largess in cattle that they expected, and for this purpose he raided his neighbours. But he was constantly harassed by attacks on his own cattle, and on the people who lived at the foot of the hill and took refuge in the chief's place when the enemy approached. His principal enemy was Matiwane, one of the chiefs whom Shaka dispossessed, and at one time he sought a counterpoise to Matiwane by offering allegiance to Shaka. But eventually, in 1827, he finally defeated Matiwane without foreign aid. Then he had to face invasion from the Griquas who came from the Cape Colony with horses and guns. He set about arming his own men, getting the fire-arms by barter, by capture, by sending young men to work in the Cape Colony and bring guns back.

He consolidated his control over his heterogeneous subjects in part by appointing his brothers and sons as headmen of villages of miscellaneous immigrants, but also by recognizing the chiefs who came with bands of followers as his subordinate authorities. By 1843 he had come to be recognized by the British as a stable element in a still disturbed situation, and he was made responsible for keeping order among his people and handing over fugitive offenders from the Cape, and paid a small salary. He was now said to be the ruler of all the land between the Orange and Caledon rivers. Successive delineations finally left him in possession of only two-thirds of the arable land that he claimed. Nevertheless the Basuto kingdom exists to this day (1977) with the name of Lesotho.

Kings whose ritual power is not taken for granted by their new subjects may take various courses. The Rwanda capture of the *abiru*, though a rare event, is not unique. The much less powerful Manganja chiefs of the Shire basin in Malawi seem to have taken over and gradually transformed through the centuries the cult of a hero called Mbona, whose shrines they found when they entered the country. The typical policy in West Africa was to form an alliance with the existing ritual leaders, the 'owners of the land' as such men are called in different languages over a wide area. Here there was no question of taking over ritual power; the political conquerors were dependent in the ritual sphere on the men who alone could communicate with the spirits of the earth, ensure the welfare of the inhabitants and make the necessary atonement if some disaster struck them. Jacques Lombard tells us what happened when Bariba immigrants from the east established their control over Borgu, in the north-east of the present Dahomey. The 'owners of the land' asserted the right to preside over the installation and funeral ceremonies of the new chiefs, the moments, as Lombard points out (1965: 183), when political stability is most precarious. An 'owner of the land' was always a member of the king's council, sometimes its most important member; he took the king's place if he was away at war, and during the period of seclusion before his enthronement. These are cases among many where the king makes no claim to be 'divine'.

But something more needs to be said about the ritual power that is ascribed to many kings. We say that ritual is symbolic, and so it is. But the use of the word tends to reinforce the spontaneous feeling of sceptics and positivists that it is somehow not 'real'. The observer is satisfied that its significance is expressive and not instrumental, but those who believe in its efficacy do hold it to be in some way instrumental; and this provides a real support for political power. The subject of a chief whose anger is held to prevent the rain from falling *really* thinks twice before challenging his claims, and this enhances the chief's *real*, secular power. All chiefs have a claim to a share in precious objects found on their domains, and it is from this that they have been able to acquire that monopoly of foreign trade which in turn makes their subjects dependent on them for valued goods. At the outset they must have relied more on the belief in ritual punishment for sacrilege than in their ability directly to punish those who did not bring them the tribute due. Godfrey Wilson (1939) showed for the tiny kingdom of Ngonde, with its area of 3,000 square miles and population of 40,000, at the head of Lake Malawi, the operation of factors that could be found at work in larger and more famous ones. The starting point here was the king's claim to one tusk of any elephant killed within his domain. This is a very common type of royal prerogative. It may be a claim to the hide of large game animals such as leopards; the petty chiefs of the Banyang in the east of Nigeria claim the whole carcass of a leopard killed in a hunt, and failure to present it is a declaration of independence (Ruel 1969). Everyone has heard that a Nuer earth-priest has the right to wear a leopard-skin over his shoulders. In many different contexts one can see the symbolic association between the power of fierce animals and ritual power, but the real political effect of ritual power is not so often emphasized.

The traditions of Ngonde tell how it has 'always' traded ivory for iron goods, which might have come from other African peoples, and cloths and 'white crockery', which could only have come from overseas. It was believed that if any hunter tried to cheat the Kyungu of his ivory he would be punished by the wrath of the royal ancestor-spirits and would never kill another elephant. This belief did effectively maintain the king's right in the low-lying country around the capital, and no doubt the foundations of his wealth were laid in that way. But in the hills of the interior the territorial chiefs were expected to receive and pass on this tribute, and if one failed to do so a force of warriors led by a prince or one of the nobles of the plain would be sent to 'burn him up'.

But those who handed over the ivory received in return gifts of the cloths for which the Kyungu bartered it, and which he distributed on other occasions as a mark of his favour; they were worn as turbans, and thus proclaimed the royal favour to all.

All these were small kingdoms—Rwanda and Lesotho nearly equal in area, each the size of Belgium, and Ngonde less than one-third as large as the other two. More questions must be asked of the 'empires', whether or not they deserve to be called 'vast', that did extend over considerable distances. How were they held together?

In writing of the Luba-Lunda 'empire', Vansina makes much of the principle of 'perpetual kinship' which was identified by Cunnison as a feature of the chiefdoms of north-eastern Zambia and Malawi. Where this is the rule, the successor to any political office is held to stand in the same kinship relation to other office-holders as his remotest ancestors did. Thus, if at one time the headmen of two villages were actually brothers, their successors for ever are said to be brothers; in other cases two village heads are linked for ever as father and son, or mother's brother and sister's son. This, as Vansina says, early linked the migrating Lunda groups into 'a loose political unit' (1966: 78). But most of the Zambian and Malawian peoples who follow this principle have never become anything more than loose political units; and I would guess that something more is needed to make political control from one centre effective.

What is needed surely is some arrangement for the maintenance of authority in those fields where the dominant population has something to gain: tribute, tolls on trade, the provision of manpower. The most banal way to secure this is of course 'indirect rule'—one of the oldest political devices in history, although it is now popularly believed to be a peculiarly wicked invention of the British. The ruler of some small unit is either defeated in battle or seeks protection, and is confirmed in his position subject to the payment of tribute and possibly also raising a fighting force when called upon. African rulers, being committed neither to economic development nor to the improvement of the morals of their subjects, did in fact leave the subject chiefs to govern in their own way much more than their European successors did.

But some other methods are interesting enough to be mentioned. 'Direct rule', the appointment of an outsider from the dominant power, is one. This was the method of Alafin Abiodun of Oyo in the late eighteenth century, when he was in competition with Dahomey for the control of communications with the coast. He placed princes or commoner or slave officials in all the towns where trading caravans used to halt, and the explorers Lander and Clapperton found that there were considerable numbers of Oyo officials concerned with the collection of tolls. He also protected his western marches against possible intrusion by sending men to colonize them.

The method of the kings of Barotseland was different again. They appointed representatives to live near the subject chiefs 'to watch over the districts for them and to forward tribute' (Gluckman 1951: 17). In addition conquered populations, along with the 'true' Lozi, were allotted to 'sectors' each under the ultimate control of a senior member of the king's council, who together with all the other councillors belonging to the sector held a court where cases between sector members were tried. In the centre of the kingdom sector membership was not based on residence, but had rather the effect of breaking up territorial groups. But conquered peoples on the periphery would be attached *en bloc* to one or other. People were summoned in sectors for war or for large-scale public works, but according to Gluckman (1951: 39) such calls were rare.

At an early period each division of the Asante state had its own war organization, with chiefs of the right, left, centre, and rearguard. But the campaigns which extended its borders all through the eighteenth century were waged by a combined force in which these four commands were held by the war chiefs of different divisions. In the course of this period it came to be accepted that the Asantehene could call on the forces of any *omanhene* (chief) to fight on his behalf.

Side by side with this reorganization of the army went the

kind of internal change that has been described earlier in this chapter. Osei Kwadwo, who succeeded in 1764, replaced the lineage heads who had traditionally formed his council by young men brought up at court; some of these, however, succeeded in asserting the right to pass on their office to their heirs. Osei Kwadwo also created a personal bodyguard; and doubtless he relied on them to enforce, as we are told he did, peace between divisions whose armies could previously have fought against one another. Like the rulers of Oyo, the Asantehene appointed officers on the trade routes who not only collected tolls but controlled entry into the kingdom.

In Asante there was a two-way communication between centre and periphery. Proconsuls, as a nineteenth-century writer called them, resident commissioners as Wilks (1967: 222) calls them, using a British title, were appointed to live at the capitals of the subject chiefs and keep an eye on them, though doubtless not possessing the executive powers that the Roman or British empires would have given them. Such commissioners were also appointed to reside at the Danish, Dutch, and British trading-posts. In addition each of the subordinate chiefs was attached to one of the officials of the Asante court who was his intermediary in dealings with the Asantehene, and who also, as Wilks (1975) interprets the record, was responsible for suppressing any attempt at rebellion that he might make.

The aim of this chapter has been to trace, where the data allow it, the steps by which the builders of kingdoms have first asserted their power in competition with rivals on their home ground and then secured their control over conquered areas, a matter which may be more difficult than the actual conquest. Inevitably at certain points it has anticipated a description of the devices by which African kingdoms were administered, but later chapters will examine these in detail.

CHAPTER III
ROYALTY AND RITUAL

EVERY African king has traditionally undergone at his accession a *rite de passage* whereby he entered on the unique status that set him apart from all his subjects, and was endowed with the qualities that he needed in order adequately to play his role. Such a rite is clearly parallel to a European coronation, and where there are still kings in Africa, no doubt there are still rites, even if they are done in the truncated form which is all that remains when a man who has adopted Christianity and had a western education ascends a throne. But much traditional ritual has gone by the board, above all that which is not connected with accession. In those African kingdoms that did not rest on Islam, rites were traditionally performed by or for a king at intervals throughout his reign. Those of southern Africa were associated with the eating of first-fruits; the most famous of these, the Swazi *incwala*, also simulated the cleavages within the kingdom and the triumph of the king over internal enemies. Some annual rites reiterated the myth of the founding of the kingdom, and these too gave their appropriate place to persons representing divergent interests. Some were directed to the renewal of the king's power, or of that of the ritual objects with which he was invested at his accession. These often involved the taking of human lives; the 'annual customs' of Dahomey are the most spectacular example.

Some kings were themselves ritual rainmakers as well as secular rulers. On the whole this is typical of those smaller states that are usually referred to by the less imposing name of chiefdoms. But the Zulu and Swazi kings make a striking exception to the rule that, with the expansion of kingdoms, there appears a pantheon of gods, each with his specialized power and each with his own priests, to whom the king sends the appropriate offerings. Mercier (1954), writing of Dahomey, convincingly explains the multiplicity of gods by the adoption of the divinities of conquered peoples, but such an explanation has not been offered in all cases. A specialist priesthood may become a counter-power to the king, as did the Yoruba diviners who annually consulted the oracles to learn whether the Oba still had the favour of the gods, a clearly political function.

A recently published short history of Africa (Oliver and Fage 1962) gathers all these different rituals and some others together in a paragraph describing 'divine kingship' as a set of customs which we are told were characteristic of ancient Egypt, and could only be found in countries so widely separated if they had all originated in a single source. Such a composite picture might be thought of as an 'ideal type', though its components are much more specific than those of a Weberian ideal type would be. It would, I think, be hard to find a complex of royal ritual that included them all. What historians have been able to trace of the founding and expansion of kingdoms, as it was summarized in the previous chapter, gives little ground for supposing that ambitious kingdom-builders carried in their luggage a blue-print from ancient Egypt. Nevertheless, some items of royal ritual are very similar to those of ancient Egypt, notably the act of real or symbolic incest between a king and his sister or mother. Certainly the association of royalty with incest, where this is regarded otherwise as a heinous offence, is a way of asserting the uniqueness of the king. But does it make him a god, if this is what it means to call him divine?

Sir James Frazer did not ascribe the origin of 'divine kingship' to Egypt, rather to a universal stage in the intellectual development of mankind. He rightly perceived that persons supposed to be endowed with more than ordinary power have more often been priests than secular rulers. But he also held that all peoples at some time believed that the life of a nation was literally embodied in its king, and that not only his death, but any diminution of his health, was directly reflected in the welfare of his country as a whole. Hence, Frazer asserts, some kings had to pass tests at regular intervals, and some were allowed to reign only for a limited time. He quotes the Yoruba kings as an example, since it was said that if the divination was unfavourable, a king could be asked to die, but he does not demonstrate that the oracle was concerned with the state of his health, and a hard-headed anthropologist might say that what was of more interest was the state of the nation. This may also be true of the many other African traditions that kings were put to death when their physical powers were failing; perhaps the national misfortune came first and was explained by the failure of the king's powers. But it is certain that the ultimate blessing, life in the fullest sense of the word, was believed by many peoples to be given them and maintained for them through the medium of a king derived from the right line of descent, and consecrated in the right manner. Indeed, kingship seems to be inseparable from the belief that the potential for rule is the possession of a particular lineage, and this to be much more fundamental than the idea of the kingdom as a material possession.

Accession Rites

Detailed accounts of accession rites show them to have a number of features in common. They all confer *power*—not divinity—on the king. They include a statement of his obligations towards his people. All the main recognized groups among his subjects co-operate in the performance of the ritual, and so commit themselves to the maintenance of the kingdom under his rule. The ritual dignifies by association with ultra-human beings a procedure analogous to the taking of a coronation oath in the presence of the peers of the realm—that too a ritual process, though we have forgotten today why an oath is supposed to be sacred.

The power that a king received at his accession was not necessarily, or wholly, a gift of wonder-working like the medieval 'royal touch', or the control of the weather that a few rulers with secular powers were believed to possess. The Alur of the Nile-Congo divide had a concept that sums up, I believe, a more general attitude. Their word for chiefship—for the status of chief—meant at the same time the qualities that a chief must have. The word was *ker*. To say that *ker* had 'become cold' meant either that an individual had proved unable to assert his authority, or that his rain ritual had been unsuccessful. To the Alur political success was no more and no less 'magical' than the powers that we should describe by that word.

No more and no less; but both kinds of power were—or it might be better to say this undifferentiated power was—held to derive from the potency of the medicines with which the king was treated and from the regalia the possession of which was essential, along with his descent status, to make his rule legitimate. It had to be kept at full strength not only by rituals to renew it in the king's person, but sometimes also by others directed to the regalia; and it was because the power was that of life in the widest sense that these rituals might involve the taking of life. Sometimes, as in the Swazi first-fruits ceremony, the king's power and the life of the nation were renewed together.

Accession rituals, like many of the puberty rituals through which ordinary people were launched on adult life, included admonitions to the new ruler on his responsibilities to his people and his kingdom. These might be made in public orations on the occasion of his installation, as they were, for example, in Asante. Or, in a closer parallel to the typical initiation ritual, the new king might spend a longer or shorter period in seclusion being instructed both in ritual and secular matters. The king of Dahomey spent a short time 'meditating on his newly acquired responsibilities in a special recess of the palace' (Lombard, 1967a: 85). The king of Parakou, one of the Bariba rulers, spent three months at the home of the chief priestess, and it was there that he performed the actions through which he cast off his previous personality, though we are not told what else occupied his time; his instruction came later on, and it seems to have consisted less in moral principles than in giving him a sort of verbal map of his kingdom showing what persons or groups had claims to particular rights or privileges. A Bariba prince, like the sons of many other African kings, was brought up away from the capital lest he should intrigue against the ruler, so that this was more than a repetition in solemn circumstances of facts that he already knew. A king-elect of Dahomey was led through a series of rooms each containing sacks of pebbles which purported to represent the population of the country, increasing in every reign, and admonished that he too must contribute to this process (Argyle 1966: 98).

The king of a Yoruba town was 'captured' in his house and

taken to the bush for instruction. He was one of many who were supposed to be so reluctant to succeed to office that they had to be seized by force. Frazer interpreted this as the very understandable misgiving of a man who knew the dangers of kingship and the likelihood that he would not be allowed to live out his days. This may have been true of some kings, particularly those who were primarily priests; something very like it is remembered of the 'divine king' of the Nyakyusa (Wilson 1959: 21). But it is as likely that the simulated reluctance was held to show that the king-elect was not (or ought not to be) an ambitious man seeking an office which he would turn to his own advantage.

Another aspect of accession ritual that has sometimes been noted shows that this possibility was much in the minds of African kingmakers. This is the kind of symbolic action which impresses on the king that he is king only by the choice of his people; something that is expressly stated in a Swazi proverb. Thus a Yoruba king-elect was beaten and dressed in rags before being inducted into the position in which his person would be sacred; without the goodwill of the elders, perhaps, the message was, he would be no higher than anybody else. Victor Turner (1969) describes, in more detail than we have for the accession ceremonies of many more powerful chiefs, a similar ritual for the Kanongesha, the senior chief of the 17,000-strong Ndembu in Zambia. The original Kanongesha was one of the leaders who extended Lunda rule so widely in central Africa, and his domains were once much wider than any he could claim now. A new Kanongesha was secluded in a small hut about a mile from the capital, where he was said to 'die', as initiands at puberty so often are. He entered the hut with a ritual wife, both of them clad in rags. They had to crouch in a posture of respect while they were treated with the medicines of chiefship, and later were ordered to do menial tasks. The 'owner of the land', the representative of the conquered people, harangued the new Kanongesha in abusive terms. He was not merely told how a chief should behave, but credited with evil ways which he must abandon in the future. Anyone who claimed to have suffered injury at his hands could come and revile him. Thus protest against the abuse of power that all men know to be its inherent danger took a more dramatic form than mere injunction. From that time on public protest would be silent.

The transition from the status of one prince among many to that of a unique ruler was marked by the usual symbols of discarding, notably head-shaving, washing and (in Bunyoro) nail-paring. Those kings who were clothed in rags during their seclusion had of course already shed their normal garments. The king of Parakou presented his prince's robes to the 'owner of the land', who shaved him in a house that he entered by one door and left by another, one more symbol of transition. This king also performed in a symbolic action that repudiation of the past which the elders demanded of the Kanongesha. He had to bestride the body of a sacrificed bull, and thereby transmit to it his whole past personality, including whatever malign influences might be attached to him. The beast was then eaten by 'the representatives of the autochthonous element'—that is the 'owner of the land' with unspecified others—who, says Lombard (1965: 326), would inherit part of the unlucky influences from which the king had been cleansed.

The procedure of installation must include some specific act that confers upon the king the legitimacy that comes from continuity with his predecessors. The most striking example is the 'possession' of the Reth of the Shilluk by his ancestor Nyikang. More often the continuity was expressed by the king's association with some material object, and sometimes this object was said to have been brought to the country by the founder of the dynasty or some famous king of the past. These regalia—'things of kingship'—both expressed and conferred on him his uniqueness, and some were publicly shown only during the accession rites. *Only* a king or queen of England may sit on the Coronation Chair, and that *only* during the ceremony of crowning; at other times it is kept in the ritual centre of the Anglican Church, Westminster Abbey. Closely resembling the Coronation Chair is the Golden Stool of Asante, the sacred shrine of the Asantehene's ancestors, in which—not in the king himself—the soul of the nation was held to reside (Rattray 1923: 290). The king never even sat on the Stool but rested his arm on it at his installation, and it was seen only at an annual ceremony.

In those states in which it was taken for granted that there would be a contest for the succession, the winner was he who held the significant emblem; and a usurper must capture it to make his conquest secure. In an interregnum it embodied the kingship. In the Interlacustrine kingdoms this most precious emblem was a drum. In Ankole the drum Bagyendanwa was supposed to have been brought to the country by the founder of the dynasty which ruled until Obote's destruction of all the kingdoms. It had its own shrine where people came with supplications, and, unlike other drums, it was never actually beaten; other drums were beaten in its honour. Ankole was one of the states where, on the death of the ruler, claimants to the throne were expected to fight it out; victory went to the one who secured control of Bagyendanwa. The Ganda royal drum could not be beaten during an interregnum; it was silent during the two years when the last Kabaka was exiled by the British government. That of Rwanda was kept in vigour by sprinkling on it the blood of animals killed for the divination ritual which preceded a war; it also was too sacred to be beaten at all. In Bunyoro a false pretender would not be able to make the drum sound when he beat it at his installation.

What might be called the constitutional aspects of installation are given especial solemnity by their association with the calling down of divine blessing on the new king. One could say of this part of the ritual what a recent writer has said of the annual renewal ceremonies of the South African Bantu: 'Representatives of the people address the ruler in a national dialogue about high office' (Sansom 1974: 261). Even though it contains a tantalizing reference to 'other ceremonies which it is unnecessary to include here', the account of his own accession ritual which was written by the last king of Bunyoro at the time of the coronation of George VI illustrates these themes in remarkably full detail ('K.W.' 1937). The public part of the ritual consisted partly in exhortations and partly in the presentation to the new king of objects which symbolized his various functions. Each of these objects, and the person presenting it, had its proper name; there is a rich field here for the study of etymology in relation to symbols. The duty and honour of making these presentations fell to representatives of different clans. On his first appearance before the assembled populace the king was 'made to swear that he will never frighten his nation, he must rule his people peacefully, he must admit foreigners to settle in his country, he must equally love his subjects however poor they may be, he must look after the orphans, and that he must justly "cut cases" (i.e. give judgments)'. The gifts included a spear (to kill rebels), a dagger and shield, both symbolizing the protection of the country, a stick and whip for minor punishments (to remind him that he should not 'frighten his nation' by inflicting savage penalties), a hoe for plentiful crops, a bow and arrows and an alarm whistle for offensive warfare, a bag made of leopard-skin (which symbolizes success in trade), and a hammer for making spears and hoes (victory and prosperity). A man representing foreigners [conquered populations?] showed him an elephant tusk which 'denotes that he is the head of all rainmakers'. Some of the objects used are said to have been handed down from the founder of the dynasty or even from remoter rulers, and some of the actors claimed descent from forebears who performed the same actions in those distant days.

Another typical address that has been preserved is the one made at the accession of an Asante chief (Rattray 1929: 82). 'Tell him', his leading subordinates say to the 'spokesman', the official through whom he communicates in public with lesser folk, 'We do not wish that he should disclose the origin of any person [since some are descended from slaves]. We do not wish that he should curse us. We do not wish greediness. We do not wish that his ears should be hard of hearing. We do not wish that he should call people fools. We do not wish that he should act out of his own head [without consultation]. We do not wish things to be done as in Kumase. We do not wish that it should ever be that he should say "I have no time". We do not wish personal violence.' This text calls for a commentary which unfortunately Rattray has not given us. The chief himself called down dire penalties 'if I with you [his subordinate chiefs] do not rule the people as well as my forefathers and you ruled them, and if I do not listen to your advice'.

Among 'refresher' rituals the most fully described is the *incwala* or first-fruits ceremony of the Swazi, which was witnessed three times and recorded by Dr. Hilda Kuper (1947), and has been interpreted and reinterpreted by later anthropologists. This renews at the same time the political power of the king and his warriors, and with it that of the nation, and the fertility of the land, which the king assures as he initiates a new year by spitting to east and west the medicines with which he has himself been treated. His political authority is strengthened even in this latter context by the belief that disaster will befall those who eat of their own harvests before he has performed the rite.

The *incwala* fell into two parts, in each of which the king was first treated with medicines and then conveyed the power they had given him to his people and country by spitting to east and west, an act that was called 'stabbing' or 'biting' the new year. The features of the ritual that have given rise to discussion are two: the fact that at certain stages in it songs expressing hatred for the king were sung, and the fact that at those same stages categories of persons who might be expected to be particularly hostile to him—namely, his own clansmen (potential rivals) and aliens not fully integrated into the Swazi polity—were excluded from parts of it. Gluckman (1954) bases on these two points a theory that this was a 'ritual of rebellion', in which the hostility that all authority must provoke was admitted and at the same time kept within the bounds of prescribed ritual behaviour. It strengthened the kingdom in the political sense by admitting the existence of conflict and then enacting the ultimate triumph of authority.

Beidelman, however (1966), interprets the *incwala* in a manner that makes it more analogous to other African 'refresher' rituals, and also disposes of the difficulty that it was *not* the people most likely to resent the royal authority who sang the hate songs; they had to be absent while the songs were sung. Was it the singers, the general populace, who were expressing hatred, when a little later, after the 'stabbing of the new year', they would be bursting into songs of praise? They did not sing 'We hate', but 'they hate'. The hate songs, as Beidelman points out, are sung while the king is being doctored, when his powers are about to be renewed to their maximum strength. Beidelman does not offer an explanation for what remains a peculiar

feature of this particular ritual. But he explains the exclusion of
the royal kin as part of the process of separation and transfor-
mation that can be seen in many rituals affecting the status of
individuals. Again, in the second phase of *incwala* the king had
to walk naked through the people, and this has been interpreted as a humiliation; this too Beidelman sees as the expression of the denial of social personality characteristic of that part
of a status ritual when the subject of it has cast off an old self
and not yet assumed a new. He does note, however, that the
warriors who were throughout closely associated with the king
were, like him, detached from divisive lineage relations and
dedicated, as he was, to the kingdom as an entity.

No other royal ritual has been directly observed and
recorded in detail by an anthropologist. The performances that
Hilda Kuper witnessed were done in 1936–8, a time when
already the great majority of such rites had been abandoned or
seriously modified. Many of the records of the past refer to the
taking of human life both in accession and refresher ceremonies, and the significance of these has been interpreted in
different ways. In the case of the Nyoro the purpose is said to
be 'to strengthen the kingship'; the life sacrificed by the subject
contributed in some way to the life of the ruler. Bradbury
(1973: 75) says of Benin that the human sacrifices there impressed upon the people the sole right of the Oba to take
human life; but this is usually the monopoly of a supreme ruler,
whether or not royal rituals involve human sacrifice. Elsewhere, however (ibid.: 50), he refers to the great increase in
such sacrifices at the time when the kingdom was losing its
power as giving 'a hint of desperation'; this would surely sug-
gest the idea of strength obtained from the lives that were
taken. The Oba's 'mystical energy', which he was expected to
deploy for the benefit of his kingdom and people, must, one
supposes, have been considered in some way to be recharged by
the lives sacrificed during the rituals. Bradbury refers also to
the Festival of the Beads at which royal and chiefly regalia
were 're-dedicated, by human sacrifice, to the common purpose'.

In the accounts of the most famous of these ceremonies, the
'annual customs' of Dahomey, little emphasis is placed on such

an interpretation. The nineteenth-century eye-witnesses were too indignant to ask the meaning of the sacrifice of captured slaves, and the anthropologist-historians of our own day have been more interested in the effect of the ritual in reinforcing secular power. J. Lombard does remark, however, that sacrifices offered to the ancestors infused the kingdom with a new spiritual force (1967a: 85). The political aspect of the ritual is apparent in the regular reaffirmation of the king's supreme authority, the display of his wealth and military power, the rewarding of those he delighted to honour. As with the Swazi eating of first-fruits, so here the ultimate supremacy of the ruler is emphasized in the prohibition of the performance of private or local rituals of any kind before the 'annual customs' had been completed. Since their overt aim was to commemorate the royal ancestors, they asserted the legitimacy of the king's descent and recalled the past glories of the kingdom. But the annual gathering at the capital of all the leading chiefs, and of many subjects bringing tribute, also had the purely secular aspect of a quasi-parliament, or, perhaps, of those courts that the Plantaganet monarchs held on the occasion of the major Christian festivals. New policies and laws were announced, political appointments made, tribute received and redistributed, military campaigns planned.

Generally such rituals not only replenished the royal power, but also gave religious sanction to the total political system, on the one hand by requiring the presence of the holders of subordinate authority and on the other by letting them participate in the renewal of the kingdom. Sometimes they re-enacted history so as to show the victory of the king over rivals, as in the Benin festival in honour of the Oba's father, when he used to defeat in a mock battle the *Uzama* or king-makers, the descendants of the elders who are believed to have brought the founder of the dynasty from Oyo.

Royal Women

Royal spouses seldom played ritual roles, but royal mothers and sisters frequently did, and at the same time exercised secular authority equivalent to that of senior chiefs. Beattie (1971: 102 ff.) describes the ceremony of appointment of the

Nyoro king's 'official sister', the Kalyota; she was presented with the characteristic insignia of office, drank milk from the royal herd and kissed the king's hand, as leading chiefs did on their appointment. Her duty was to keep the peace among the women of the royal clan, and, like the other chiefs, she had an official estate—an area of land over which she exercised authority in just the same manner as they did. The Ganda and Ankole also recognized a royal sister, and also a royal mother (so did the Nyoro, but Beattie tells us little about her). These were offices which had to be filled; they were essential to the continuance of the monarchy. Each king at his accession installed his own mother and chose his official sister, but if the royal mother died before her son—as was most likely—a substitute was installed in her place. The royal mother in Ankole wielded considerable secular power. She was a member of her son's council, her consent was necessary before anyone could be put to death, and envoys from foreign rulers had to approach her before they could see the king.

In these kingdoms it had traditionally been the rule that succession to the throne was decided by a war between the potential heirs in which the defeated were eliminated; hence, in theory, the king had no brothers, and in practice he would have been unlikely to have relations of confidence with them. Oberg (1940: 160) suggests that his closest female kin gave him the advice and support that other rulers got from their male agnates, but there is really no reason why he should not have looked to men on his mother's side, and he did have a 'favourite councillor' or 'prime minister' whom he chose for himself.

Moreover, royal mothers and sisters figure in kingdoms where there is no question of the elimination of the king's brothers. In the Lozi kingdom, as described by Gluckman (1951), the 'princess chief' controlled the most potent of all royal shrines, the grave of the king Mwanambinji, who seized from a conquered enemy the drums that became the major insignia of kingship.

In the Hausa kingdom of Maradi, a royal lady, not necessarily the king's mother, was appointed to preside over rituals involving royal women. She was the official head of the prostitutes, a recognized profession in Muslim societies, and also of the adepts of the pagan *bori* spirit possession cult. She had a say in all public rituals. She had her own slaves and clients and her own armed following which went to war at her command; she collected market tolls and taxes from the prostitutes. In Oyo not only the Alafin but every official in the palace had his 'mother'; these women had ritual responsibility for the palace shrines, and the most important of them were also 'mothers' of the principal city-wide cult organizations. The Alafin's own official mother had to be with him whenever he gave audience to one of his chiefs, and the heir apparent, the king's eldest son, had to be accompanied by *two* 'mothers' when he visited the palace (Morton-Williams 1967: 65).

The capital of Dahomey was similarly organized. According to Burton every man at the court had an official mother, and other writers confirm that this was so in the case of the two leading officials, the *migan* or prime minister and the *meu* or war chief. These ladies had authority over the great number of women who inhabited the palace, the first over commoners, the second over royal women. As in Oyo, a minister's 'mother' had to be present when he was in conference with the king. European visitors to Dahomey had 'mothers' attached to them for the same purpose. It was their responsibility to remember what had been said at the audiences.

From the meagre information that we have about these royal sisters and mothers it seems that most of them exercised some kind of secular authority, and the question may be asked why they should be discussed in the context of ritual. Where we are concerned with great concourses of women far exceeding the numbers to be found in any ordinary household (nearly 8,000 in Dahomey), it is merely common sense to observe that some authority among them must have been necessary, and that this could more appropriately be vested in a woman than a man. But this does not account for all the cases in which a sister or mother 'reigns with' her son or brother, nor for the fact that a king's wife *never* does so; and those writers who have discussed the subject agree that the institution had a symbolic as well as a practical significance, though they are by no means unanimous as to what this was. It need not, of course, be the same in all cases, just as the role of the sister or mother was not the same everywhere.

Argyle (1966: 64) associates the Dahomeyan institution with the opposition that was recognized between the 'inside'—the palace—and the 'outside'—the rest of the kingdom. The 'mothers' of the ministers and of other visitors to the court paralleled in their secluded feminine world the men of affairs whose activities were carried on outside. But in addition, there was a need for some mediating term between the king 'inside' and his ministers 'outside', and this was supplied by the official 'mothers'. This explanation might apply also to Oyo, where there was a similar division between palace and town, and the Alafin was supposed never to leave the palace.

But these women's motherhood was no more than metaphorical, and they present a different problem from that of the mothers and sisters who were expressly stated to 'reign with' a king. The explanation of their status which has been offered by Luc de Heusch (1958) turns on the theory that most African accession rituals include an incestuous marriage which may involve a real or symbolic act of incest. His prototype case is that of the Nyoro Kalyota, whose ritual of installation was described by Roscoe as a marriage; Beattie's discussion of this rite shows that it does not at all closely parallel a Nyoro marriage. However, de Heusch adduces many more cases in support of his argument than have been cited here. He maintains that for the king to be not only permitted but enjoined to commit incest—an act regarded among ordinary folk as abhorrent—emphasizes his uniqueness in the most extreme manner possible. It also, by making the incestuous union a *marriage*, combines concepts that are diametrically opposed. And by doing this it sacralizes sexual relations, and so fertility, throughout the kingdom. Monarchy, says de Heusch, is here founded on the sacred triad of king, sister, and mother.

Beattie (1971: 103), after he has effectively demonstrated that there was no rite of incestuous marriage in Bunyoro, rather dodges the issue by simply saying that the queen-sister's role is 'as the female expression or counterpart of the kingship'. This theme is developed by Balandier (1974) in a discussion of the various ways in which the opposition and complementarity of the sexes are perceived in Afrrican societies. For him the queen-sister's authority over other women is the essential of her position, and he compares her with the queen-mothers of smaller African kingdoms in Cameroun. In the Nyoro case the queen-mother, the third in the triad, is said to 'protect' the king, though it is not entirely clear what this means. But if it is a matter of magical rites, Balandier argues, the two royal women, who together represent the 'feminine society', are then differentiated and opposed in terms of the complementary opposition between sacred and secular power. Balandier's explanation does not invoke the symbolism of fertility. He stresses rather the assimilation of these female chiefs to men: 'When I go into council', said a princess chief to Gluckman, 'I change; I am a man'. As the West African 'mothers' mediate between the palace and the 'outside', so the de-feminized female chiefs effect a 'marriage' between the two sides in the basic, ineluctable division between the sexes.

CHAPTER IV

COURTS AND CAPITALS

No anthropologist has been in a position to write an eye-witness account of an independent African court or capital. But it has been possible to piece together from the records of travellers and the memories of old men a reasonably satisfactory picture of some of them.

Different writers have concentrated on different aspects. Evans-Pritchard (1971) put together a pretty full description of the court of Gbudwe, the last independent Zande king, by combining travellers' accounts, texts taken from old men who had been royal soldiers or pages when they were young, and what he could see himself in 1927 of the diminished splendour of Gbudwe's son. R. E. Bradbury spent six years in Benin and collected both documents and oral traditions as part of a project for a history of the kingdom; he died before he could publish a full-scale ethnography, but he has given us an admirable picture of palace organization. Beattie (1971) describes the numerous officials, many with purely ritual functions, to be found at the relatively unelaborate court of the king of Bunyoro; the prestige attached even twenty years ago to such offices was often sufficient to prevent their holders from seeking more lucrative employment elsewhere. M. G. Smith, more interested in political processes than in descriptive detail, used for his description (1960) of Zazzau (now called Zaria) a chronicle of nineteenth-century Abuja, the kingdom founded by the Hausa ruler of Zazzau when he fled from the Fulani conquest, which was made by the brother of the then Emir of Abuja; to this he added a history of the Fulani state of Zaria recounted to him by a grandson of the conqueror and some other elders.

Every court or capital comprised a greater complex of buildings and a larger population than would be found elsewhere in the king's dominions. There was therefore need for a category of officials concerned specifically with its organization and provisioning. Buganda had a king's cook and butcher: actually important men holding hereditary offices, whose duty it was to procure the necessary supplies of meat and vegetable food. Some kings also had ritual specialists who were responsible for foreseeing and warding off danger. Every king had great numbers of wives—women who had been given to him but did not necessarily become his consorts, were servants of his actual wives and might be given by him to favoured subjects. The women's quarters had their own authorities responsible both for supplies and the maintenance of order. Most kings had elaborate regalia for the upkeep of each of which, again, a specific official was responsible. In addition the highest political authorities under the king would have their residences at the court or in the capital.

Zande kings and princes still had their courts when Evans-Pritchard was there in 1927. Though it was but a shadow of what it had been in the days of Gbudwe's greatness, his son's court had the traditional lay-out. The buildings were round mud huts with thatched roofs, as were most of those of eastern and central Africa, but within this limitation there is room for considerable difference in elegance of construction and attention to upkeep. The public part of the court was an open space where people who came to present petitions or have cases judged could sit in the shade of some large tree. About twenty yards from the open court was the 'court of whispers', an unwalled building where the king would discuss secret business with his intimates. Along the path which connected the two were the houses of the royal pages, who could bar the entrance of unauthorized persons to the 'court of whispers'; and on one side of the open court were housed the military companies. The actual dwelling place of the king and his wives would be separated from this complex by a space of grassland. They covered a large area, in the case of King Gbudwe 'several miles' (Evans-Pritchard 1971: 77). Here there was a separate homestead for every wife with a garden round it, and one for the king himself somewhere in the middle. Behind this complex, at some distance, was a hut where the royal diviners consulted the poison oracle on his behalf.

Oberg (1940), who about 1935 reconstructed a picture of an

independent Nkole king's capital, follows the missionary Roscoe (1923) in calling it a 'kraal'. Earlier writers meant by this word an enclosure for cattle, later ones what might be thought of as a large homestead or a small village; it always implies the presence of cattle, and this makes it seem appropriate for the residence of the Nkole king, who was the owner of a large herd and moved with it from place to place. Oberg describes the capital as itself consisting of a number of kraals, each apparently a cluster of huts with a fence round them. The royal residence was in the centre, its gateway always guarded. In the open space inside the gate the king received visitors and suppliants and tried minor cases. But what might be called the throne-room and audience chamber, comparable to the Zande 'court of whispers', was a large hut in which serious matters of state were discussed and cases of murder and treason were tried. This was also a centre of public ritual; the installation of a new king took place in front of it. Around it were smaller huts where guests could sleep, and one to store the beer that was always offered for their refreshment. A large enclosure housed the women of the court. This was subdivided into quarters for favourite wives, for concubines, for immature girls who might or might not become royal consorts; a girl chosen by the king was fattened by being made to drink enormous quantities of milk while living in a special hut set apart for the purpose.

Outside this royal residence were the dwellings of court officials and servants. According to the Nkole historian S. R. Karugire (1971) the closest to the royal enclosure were those of regional chiefs, who were also war leaders, and who, like most of their counterparts elsewhere, were expected to show their loyalty by spending much of their time in the capital. Commoner chiefs were nearest the king's quarters; princes, who might harbour thoughts of assassination, further away. At an equal distance in a different direction lived the ambassadors/hostages of conquered rulers. Oberg does not describe any cattle enclosure within this complex, and Karugire says the royal herd was kept some distance away.

It has commonly been from among the palace attendants, whose qualities and loyalty the king could judge at first hand, that the holders of political office were chosen, so that the

question of their recruitment and promotion is of some significance. From the kingdoms of Uganda we get the general impression that men would send their sons to serve at court as
pages in the hope of launching them on successful careers; in
particular fathers who were themselves chiefs would do so.

According to one of Evans-Pritchard's informants, Kuagbiaru, who had been a royal page and then a warrior, a
Zande king would himself pick out the boys whom he wanted.
There is an apparent contradiction in a later statement that
boys chose to serve at court because the king would provide
their bridewealth. It may be, of course, that they or their
fathers were free to refuse the royal invitation and that this was
a motive for accepting it. In any case the poison oracle was
consulted to find whether the invitation was propitious, and an
unfavourable answer might be held to justify a refusal.

A select number of pages were the king's constant compan-
ions, and the youngest of these were allowed to enter his domestic quarters, from which all other males were excluded.
Hence they might learn a good deal about his private affairs,
and the first requirement of such a confidential follower was
the ability to keep his mouth shut. These pages went with the
king to court, to war, to a hunt, to consult the poison oracle or
on a journey, and slept within earshot so that he could summon
them at will. Pages guarded the entrance to the 'court of whispers' and kept out those who had no right of access to it. They
carried out into the public place the huge bowls of food that
were prepared every day for all the men at the court. They
were sent with messages, and were also expected to be spies.
Kuagbiaru said the king told them: 'Anything you may hear
anyone say about me, do not hide it from me in any circumstances. You must know the names of everybody who attends
court, for if I ask you who is in the court you must be able to
name every one of them correctly' (Evans-Pritchard 1971:
184). Older pages shared in the work of hoeing the king's
extensive fields, where the grain was grown that provided for
the lavish distribution of food and beer, and younger ones
might help the royal wives, who had each her garden like other
Zande women. They were threatened with ferocious punishment for any dereliction of duty, and, according to Kuagbiaru,

when a prince died all his pages at the time were put to death.

The greatest elaboration of courts and capitals was naturally to be found in those West African kingdoms—some call them empires—that were built on the control of trade. We know more of Asante than of any other, thanks to the records of visitors to Kumase at different times in the nineteenth century. But it is from Rattray, the Gold Coast Government Anthropologist in the period between the two world wars, that we learn just what kind of a labyrinth the residence of a royal personage might be. When Rattray was at work, the Asantehene had recently been allowed to return, as a private citizen, from a long exile, and his studies of the nature of Asante kingship were made by visiting the different chiefs and collecting their versions of remembered history. When with the chief of Kumawu he drew a plan of the palace there and numbered each of the separate rooms according to its use. Asante buildings were rectangular, with mud walls and roofs which in the present century are made of corrugated iron or thatched with straw, but earlier had been of leaves stitched together. This palace was a large rectangle the external wall of which consisted of rooms divided by partitions, while inside there were courtyards and free-standing buildings.

The entrance was at a corner, not in the middle of a wall. Since the most striking item of a chief's insignia was the large umbrella carried over his head, the doorway had to be wide enough for one of these to pass through. Immediately inside was the open court where the chief held audience and tried important cases. This was called *gyase*, a word that refers to the cooking-hearth and the space around it where, in ordinary houses, women and servants work and children play. Domestic slaves slept there, and were called *gyasefo*, 'people of the hearth-place', and in a large establishment one was set in authority over the rest as *gyasehene*. This, therefore, was the title given to the official in charge of the multitude of servants in the king's vast household. At the further side of the *gyase* was an open-fronted room where on important occasions the chief would sit and serve out wine. Opposite him was the room where his drummers sat, and, on the two other sides of the square, rooms where the drums were kept. In a smaller court leading out of this to the right he dealt with cases among his own servants; only members of his household had access there. It was flanked by his bathroom and rooms for his bath attendants, who in this case were also cooks, and his youngest servants. To the left, separated by a wall, was the court where lived the *Barimhene*, the official responsible for the ceremonies that commemorate the chief's ancestors, whose souls were believed to be enshrined in the stools that they had sat on in their life-time, which were blackened and kept in a shrine-house when they died. A chief himself, the *Barimhene* had his own stool-house. The Kumawuhene's stools were in a court to which there was access both from this and from the *gyase* court. Along the outer wall of this were dwellings for those responsible for the care of the stools and for menial services during the rites. In the middle was a place for heralds and musicians to sit at ceremonies, and at the further end a room containing the skeletons of dead chiefs and one for the chief to sit during rituals directed to them. Behind the *gyase* was another court where 'all the lesser ordinary' cases were tried; the chief sat on one side and his two leading subordinates opposite, and his 'linguists' at the further end. Further back was the room where the chief ate, and in front of it a small space where visitors were given food and drink. Across from this was the room where the chief slept; this looked out on an open space flanked by a room for wives who came to visit him and store-rooms for his clothes and eating utensils. Further back again was another large court, at one side of which was a room for the chief to be alone, and one near it for wives who came to see him. At the back of this were a number of store-rooms, each of which was intended for particular classes of object; but from the photographs that Rattray took it would seem that the rule 'A place for everything and everything in its place' was not strictly adhered to. At one side of this court were kept the chief's magical charms. Parallel with this court was a small one for private discussions between the chief and his elders; at one side of this the state umbrellas were kept, at another the goldsmiths in his service did their work. Here there was yet another small room for the chief to sit and rest in and 'hear complaints from his wives'. A narrow passage led from the *gyase* court to a wide space 'where small boys attending the chief's wives play', and from this there was a way into the women's area, houses along the whole interior of the side wall, garden patches along the whole of the back. Behind the room with the skeletons of dead chiefs, outside the main wall but close to it, was one for the relics of dead wives of chiefs.

The city of Kumase was divided into seventy-seven named wards, some of which were the homes of the king's servants, including those of his leading councillors, the senior of whom, the *Gyaasewahene* or treasurer, held a court of his own. His house was close to the entrance of the palace on the west, and the head of the executioners and police lived immediately to the south of the palace. Most other senior officials also lived close to the palace. The 1,000 or so Muslim merchants and mallams had their own wards; so did the goldsmiths, while the blacksmiths and umbrella-makers lived in two small hamlets outside the city. Whether inside or outside the palace, every person holding any kind of public authority had an open room facing the street, in front of his domestic dwellings, where he transacted business. One way of establishing a claim to a hereditary office up to quite recent times was to demonstrate that an ancestor had had such a *dampan*.

The palace of the kings of Dahomey at Abomey epitomized the history of the kingdom, since every king was buried in his house in the capital, and his successor had to build a house next to it. It was therefore a ritual as much as a political centre, and this may be one reason why the palace as 'the inside' was expressly opposed to all that was 'outside', and this opposition was conceived in terms of the opposition of the sexes, a leading theme in Dahomey religion. In the late nineteenth century it was estimated to have 8,000 inhabitants, the great majority being the royal wives and their slaves, who here worked the gardens and fetched water. Even the king's bodyguard were women, the 'Amazons' of whom Burton and others wrote. Senior officials were generally eunuchs; not all of them actually lived in the palace. One had the duty of making the king's path straight by removing sticks and stones in front of him, and was also in charge of the palace night-watchmen. Another controlled entry to the palace and dealt with misdemeanours among the other eunuchs. A third was in charge of the royal stores, including 'cloth, cowries and rum', and ammunition. The palace was conceived as a sort of mirror of the rest of the kingdom; within it there was for every chief who had responsibilities of government a 'mother' whose title corresponded to his own, and who was present whenever he had audience of the king. When the king appeared in public, a line was drawn on the ground by laying down bamboo sticks, which no one from the 'outside' might cross.

Again, in Oyo, the senior of the Yoruba kingdoms, the leading court officials were three eunuchs. They, however, had responsibilities outside as well as within the palace. One was responsible for the ritual of the god of thunder and could curse offenders in his name. One judged disputes between vassals of Oyo, and the third, who went to battle in the place of the king, also had authority over the collection of tolls. Actual daily duties were largely performed by slaves.

The most complex palace organization of which we have record is that of Benin. Here the palace was divided on the ground into three sections, each the residence (though not the home) of a different association of officials. In the administration of palace affairs each of these had a different sphere of responsibility. The *Iwebe*, the highest in rank, had charge of the throne and of the Oba's ceremonial garments and other insignia, and their head chief was the senior palace official; they were also responsible for his stock of trade goods. The *Iweguae* was the section of the palace where the Oba lived. Its association provided pages, messengers, domestic spies, cooks, and other servants, and it was to its members that individuals addressed themselves when they wanted a private audience with the Oba. They organized the feasts at which the Oba entertained his chiefs. In this part of the palace were stored the medicines and other magical objects used in rituals to protect the king's health and maintain his power, though the experts who manipulated them lived outside in the town. Then came the *Ibiwe*, where the Oba's wives and children lived. The *Ibiwe* chiefs were responsible for the provisioning of this large population, for keeping the peace among them and reporting on them to the Oba; and also for buying animals for sacrifices. When the wives were sick or pregnant they were taken to the home of some *Ibiwe* chief outside the palace; in such homes, too, the princes were brought up, since they were sent away from the palace as soon as they could leave their mothers. Palace chiefs had charge of the different wards of the town, some of which were allotted to the practitioners of the different crafts which supplied the palace. They were not maintained directly from the Oba's resources, but had allotted to them villages from which they drew tribute and labour, and over which they exercised the same authority as any territorial chief. Nor were their duties confined to palace affairs; they were constantly being sent, as the Oba's emissaries, to summon levies from villages other than their own, to deal with complaints, and to represent the Oba, who was expected to take part directly or indirectly in all village rituals.

The division in Benin between 'inside' and 'outside'—here called 'Palace' and 'Town'—was associated with the supposed foreign origin of the ruling dynasty; the kings were reminded in various ways that they were not wholly members of the Edo population who were their subjects. While the Palace Chiefs were first and foremost retainers of the Oba, the Town Chiefs were thought of as spokesmen for the people at large. One of them, the *Esogban*, was the 'elder' of the whole kingdom, maintaining on its behalf the same ritual relations with the dead that fell in each village to the actual oldest man. The shrine at which he officiated stood immediately outside the palace, across the broad highway that separated it from the town. Thus it confronted the shrines of dead Obas, which were directly behind the front wall of the palace. The town chiefs included the war leaders and the principal ritual functionaries of the kingdom, but we do not read of specialized administrative offices attached to their position.

The Career open to Talents

Earlier it was argued that an essential element in the consolidation of central power was the assertion by a ruler of the right to choose his subordinates without regard to hereditary claims, and oral traditions often name the ruler who first did this. He had of course to make the choice from those known to him, and in the nature of things these were most likely to have been court servants, though no doubt chiefs of lower rank might sometimes commend a follower to him. The belief that any free man—and sometimes any slave too—could rise to the highest office if he had the luck to be noticed by his superiors, and the merit to deserve their notice, was current in many African kingdoms; stories were told to illustrate it, and here and there it is supported by authentic life-histories.

It is usual to find that fathers could offer their sons as servants to their immediate chiefs, if not to the king himself, and that these authorities or their emissaries on their travels could pick out likely lads for court service. A most striking example of theoretically open access to high office was to be found in Benin, where every free man inherited from his father membership in one of the three palace associations. As with many such rights, only those could exercise it who could afford to do so. But quite a number did 'enter the palace', and stay there until they gave up hope of preferment and went back to their villages; young men from the capital, one suspects, less often had to give up hope. The three associations (*otu*) were similar in structure to the cult and other associations which have been described among the Ibo-speaking peoples; the latter have many characteristics in common with the Edo-speakers of Benin and the surrounding country. One entered any such association by paying fees to the existing members. Everyone had the right to enter his father's *otu*, but it was possible to transfer later on, and brothers were not usually found in the same *otu*; hence there was no concentration of lineages in any association. On entry a new member was given seven days' instruction in his duties and swore to be loyal to the king and not divulge court secrets; and evidently there were also rites of initiation. He then became the servant of higher-ranking members of the association. By making more payments and taking part in further rites he advanced through a series of grades to that of messenger, when he would be sent, by this time no doubt with followers of his own, on various missions on behalf of the king.

When he reached this grade he had the right to apply for one of the limited number of titles to which were attached certain villages as 'fiefs' or sources of tribute and labour. The titles did not carry specific responsibilities. They were ranked in order, but there was no ladder of promotion; anyone of the appropriate grade could apply to the Oba for any title that became vacant. Again he had to pay fees to the other title-holders and ask their blessing one by one, just as a man in the village wishing to be promoted to elderhood (still) makes gifts to each of the elders and seeks their blessing. His title was not confirmed until he had been formally installed by the senior Town chief (the *Iyase*); so there could be many a slip before he actually entered upon it. Promotion was, then, an expensive business; but every advancement brought with it more sources of wealth. Town titles were sometimes given to men who had not passed through the palace ranks but had acquired wealth as traders or craftsmen, or distinguished themselves in war; this was the background of several who held the position of *Iyase*.

The annals of Asante are full of records of the creation of new chiefships—stools—which seem to have sometimes been treated as hereditary. On the other hand, from Bowdich's time onwards, we hear how the Asantehene 'raised his favourite captains to the vacant stools, uniting three or four in one', and 'extend[ed] his prerogative by dignifying the young men brought up about his person' (cited Wilks 1975: 445). Bonnat in 1870 noticed how young men came to Kumase to offer their services in the hope of advancement. Bowdich recorded one individual success story, that of Asante Agyei. He worked in the salt trade on the Volta and was noticed by the chief of Akwamu, who enlisted him in his bodyguard. He was in the chief's retinue when the latter was summoned to Kumase to answer some charge against him. He spoke for three hours, so it is said, in defence of his master, and so impressed the Asantehene that he took him over as a retainer. Eventually he achieved another triumph in a negotiation between the Asantehene and some councillors who opposed his views, upon which he was appointed to the rank of *okyeame*, a word translated as 'linguist' by the older writers and 'counselor' (*sic*) by Wilks. He again supported a minority view in defence of a chief whom the king proposed to despoil of his property, and, surprisingly enough, was yet further advanced for this. Next he was sent with an army against the rebel chiefdom of Akyem, as the civilian responsible for concluding the peace terms, and from then on was entrusted with all negotiations with foreign states.

Equally impressive is the story of Opoku Frefre, who as Gyaasewahene (treasurer) was one of the Asantehene's four 'privy councillors', and whom Bowdich described as holding every day 'a sort of exchequer court'. According to the Asantehene Prempeh II 'Opoku Frefre had no family. He was a slave' (Wilks 1975: 461). He went to court in the retinue of one of the Kumase chiefs and was noticed by the Asantehene, who had him taken into court service as part of the share of his master's estate due to be paid as 'death duty'. He was attached to the then Gyaasewahene, and when the latter was executed for treason he was appointed in his place; he was then about thirty. He commanded armies in campaigns against rebellious southern provinces and was one of the two officials who took charge of the capital when the Asantehene was away.

CHAPTER V
ARMY ORGANIZATION

NEARLY every African people had some form of military organization.

There is an obvious contrast between those kingdoms in which soldiers were raised locally and fought as bands from their home area under a territorial chief, and those in which they were amalgamated and then divided on some other than a territorial basis; and another between those in which a 'citizen army' was summoned from its everyday avocations when it was needed, and those in which some men at least were given a special training. It might be expected that the contrast would be associated with that between the 'empires' of Zande and Luba type, in which members of a royal lineage set out on their independent conquests and recognized only a nominal supremacy of the descendants of the original head, and those in which the conquests were additions to the domains of a single ruler. But this does not always hold good. The kings of Asante, for example, although they claimed the right to demand troops from any of the chiefdoms that acknowledged their rule, also allowed some of these to raise their own armies and prosecute their own wars.

The Zande organization is the most informal to have been described in any detail. Zande warriors were unmarried youths who were recruited into companies in each of the districts administered by a representative of the king, either a prince of his own family or a commoner governor; each of these had its own commander, one of their number and so not an official with any authority outside his own company. There was no compulsion to join a company, though the young men's fathers maintained that they offered their sons' services as a form of tribute. According to Evans-Pritchard, however, it was the youths themselves who insisted on joining the companies, and their fathers could not prevent them (1971: 198). When not required for fighting, they could be called on to work the king's extensive fields; they were summoned through their local commanders. Each company had a barracks—a single very large hut—at the royal or provincial court, where the commander spent most of his time, while the others came and went, but were not expected to stay away for long periods. Individuals left when they wanted to marry. Married men joined companies in their own districts. When fighting was called for all able-bodied men, not only members of the companies, were expected to take part. Each one brought with him a spear and shield, but only the companies had the many-bladed throwing-knife, a weapon issued by kings and governors to their followers. A king also distributed additional spears to favoured warriors.

Zande warfare, as described by Evans-Pritchard, did not have the conquest of territory as its aim but simply the destruction of the enemy's possessions; movable goods were looted, women and children made captive, huts and storehouses destroyed. Captured weapons were brought to the king, and were one source from which he supplied his warriors in later campaigns. In Evans-Pritchard's view the material gains were less important to the Azande than the lowering of the enemy's prestige. But warfare was not confined to the single raids which the rulers of provinces were free to mount on their own; what they called 'sit-down' wars might last several weeks. Yet these wars, though they were fought between rival Zande kings and princes, were not, it seems, intended to establish or restore the political authority of any one of them. Auspicious times for attack were found by consulting the poison oracle, but also by spies who would report when an enemy population was preparing a feast and could be caught off guard. There were famous spies; some were named to Evans-Pritchard.

From the point of view of organization what is interesting is the supply of provisions for large numbers of men away from home. The warriors brought an initial supply with them, and those who were not too far from their homes went back for more when they needed it. In addition they might 'live on the country', even one which they were supposed to be defending. Each man foraged for himself. Evans-Pritchard refers to famines caused by the demands of Zande armies.

The centralization of the Rwanda army has been mentioned. The army organization created for the Zulu by Dingiswayo and Shaka resembled it in some respects, though its starting-point was a different one, the principle common to so many African peoples that all young men must pass through a period as 'warriors' immediately after their formal initiation into manhood. As with the Azande, it was the youths of one territorial division who fought together when their leaders summoned them. In southern Africa chiefs took charge of the initiation process, and a son of the chief would be made a leader in each of the 'regiments'—the word that has been favoured by South African writers for more than a century—that were formed in this way. In time of peace the men lived in their own, not necessarily contiguous, homes, but they fought as a body when their leader summoned them. They could be, therefore, a source of support in power struggles and so of division within the realm, as the Zande companies certainly were. Evans-Pritchard argues that what others might call internecine wars were the expression of loyalties to the immediate superior, and one which assured the maintenance of his authority. It is part of his argument that the Zande did not seek territorial expansion at one another's expense; any of them who did must surely have been driven along the same path as Dingiswayo and Shaka.

The first modification in the common type of organization was made by the former. He gave up the initiation ceremonies, supposedly because of the danger of enemy attacks when numbers of young men were away in the bush, and instead left it to his chiefs to assemble youths of the right age and give each set a regimental name. But they did not remain under local command. Each regiment was assigned a rallying-point at one of the royal households which were distributed over the country, and here age-mates from different areas collected and went to battle together. Shaka made the regiments into a standing army. They now lived in six settlements, some of them very large; one was reported to contain 1,400 huts (Isaacs, cited Omer-Cooper 1966: 34). Each was commanded by a commoner appointed by Shaka. No man could marry until the king disbanded his regiment. They spent much of their time in

military exercises. Shaka introduced the use of a short spear for
stabbing in place of the assegai which left the soldier defenceless
as soon as he had thrown it; he employed his own blacksmiths
to make these. Shields as well as spears, and all military insignia, were issued by him; another means of centralization. The
regiments were trained to manoeuvre in close formation. A
division of the royal herd was attached to each to supply them
with meat and milk; the warriors were responsible for herding
them. During the short period of Shaka's despotism he employed his army not only in the conquest and devastation of the
neighbouring country but also in the massacre of any subjects
whom he suspected of disloyalty.

The Asante empire consisted originally in an alliance of Twi-
speaking peoples, each under its own chief, who looked to the
chief of Kumase for leadership and regarded him as ritually
supreme; hence his title, Asantehene, head of Asante. Each
chiefdom had its own fighting force, but they accepted the
obligation to join in the Asantehene's wars; failure to do so, like
failure to pay tribute, constituted rebellion. All armies were
organized on the same principle; there was a right and left
wing, a centre and a rearguard (obviously a very usual form of
organization). The special feature of Asante was that the commander of each of these divisions was a hereditary official, and
the titles describing their commands were the same in every
division. Bowdich wrote in 1819 that when contingents were
raised from different chiefdoms, each was given one of these
positions and its supreme commander held the appropriate
title. But by 1870, when British military intelligence was interested in Asante armies, these commands were held by Asante
chiefs, not those of non-Asante subjects. A force of 20,000 attacked the coastal peoples twice in the nineteenth century, and
that which fought the British in 1873-4 was estimated at
60,000, the same number that the Emperor Charles V in 1539
planned to launch against the Turks.

From the beginning of the expansion of Asante, quotas of
men were imposed on conquered chiefs. According to Bowdich
a contingent from the most recently conquered people formed
the vanguard in the next campaign. Another way to obtain
soldiers was the mass transfer of conquered populations. Dis-

satisfaction with demands for troops was one reason why so many chiefs threw off their allegiance to Kumase after its defeat in 1874. But even after this, some chiefs were required to hand over slaves for the small standing army, equipped with modern weapons, that was created as a *corps d'élite*.

When the Asantehene was preparing for war in 1873, the two captive missionaries in Kumase whom the British mission had come to rescue (among other aims) noticed people drying corn and cassava and making up packages. Bowdich observed that every soldier had a bag in which he carried his rations. But unlike the Zande armies with their campaigns of a few weeks, Asante troops were often in the field for many months, and their wars were financed by the expenditure of the gold dust which was collected in tribute and by various forms of taxation. Halfway through the war of 1873–4, the Asantehene informed his council that it had cost the equivalent of £48,000 at the rate then current. Ten times as much was lost in an earlier defeat when the treasure chest was captured. A large part of these funds must have been expended on arms and ammunition; some, perhaps, on securing the support of allies or safe passage through a neutral chiefdom. Brodie Cruickshank, writing in 1853 of a war fought in 1806, refers to a chief who 'undertook to sell provisions to the Ashantee army, provided they came to his town without their arms' (1966: 66–7); and Reindorf, the Ghanaian historian, wrote of 'ammunition' spent in buying provisions (1966: 127). Conquered towns were destroyed. Cruickshank and Reindorf describe famine in the wake of Asante armies; Wilks refers to famines in Asante caused by the diversion of man-power from cultivation, something that is not mentioned in accounts of any other army.

As at all times when weapons were relatively ineffective and sanitary notions rudimentary, the heavy losses in campaigns were due as much to epidemics as to casualties in battle. A count of the number of troops under arms was 'ascertained or preserved in cowries or coins'. Ramseyer and Kühne, the captive missionaries, wrote that on returning from a battle 'every chief who passed before the king threw into a vase as many grains of corn as he had lost people' (cited Wilks 1975: 81). This was evidently a long-established method of computation, for an Arab gold dinar was reckoned to weigh 72 such grains. The Asante authorities knew the estimated strength of each province; this was reported by intelligence to the British in 1873.

Dahomey was famous for its 'Amazons', the women soldiers who were recruited by summoning to the royal palace on a fixed day the daughters of all the king's subjects and choosing those who looked most promising from among them (Skertchly 1874, cited Argyle 1966: 87). They were actually a bodyguard, necessarily female since only women lived in the palace, and there are varying accounts of them, some saying that they rarely went to war, others that they had done so from the early eighteenth century. There were two war captains, of the right and left wing, with their female counterparts. Leaders of local groups brought their followers with them, and these were combined in different ways, but the groups themselves do not seem to have been broken up as were the corresponding ones among the Zulu.

War was as normal a part of the routine of Dahomey as planting and harvesting the crops. A campaign was fought every year. The word for 'war' meant 'man-hunt' (Argyle 1966: 81), and its sole purpose was the taking of captives, which had a ritual as well as a material purpose since many were put to death at the great annual festival—the 'Customs'—so that their blood should 'water the graves' of the king's ancestors. For these ritual reasons a territory was not held to have been effectively conquered until its king had been killed. The Dahomeyan spies had magical rather than practical functions; their duty was to destroy the power of the spirits on whom the enemy relied for protection.

It was only the kingdoms on the borders of the Sahara that could employ cavalry; on the one hand horses are effective only in open country, and on the other they cannot live where diseases carried by the tsetse fly are endemic. Horses, unlike soldiers, consume food, even in peace time, which they do not help to produce (since sub-Saharan Africa did not know the plough). A description of the cavalry force of the short-lived (1818–62) Fulani empire of Masina, in the interior delta of the Niger, tells us that there were mounted soldiers in all the principal towns, as many as 10,000 at the capital. The whole population was liable to serve in the army—not all, of course, in the cavalry. Horsemen were given an allowance for weapons and harness, and on campaigns they had rations for themselves and their horses, and an allowance of food was given their families; so that the generalization that cavalry fighting must create an aristocracy because of the high cost of gear and horses does not seem to hold good here. Smiths and leather-workers went with the army on campaigns. Although the numbers of the horses themselves could be kept up and increased through war captures, the food had to come from home production, and it was largely grown by the slaves who fell to the share of the royal treasury in the distribution of spoils (Johnson 1975).

CHAPTER VI

INTERNAL ORGANIZATION

As soon as an appreciable area comes to be controlled from a single centre, problems arise of the delegation of authority; and where the control is extended over populations already organized in states, the new ruler has to decide whether he will leave the existing one in a vassal relationship, get rid of him altogether, or exercise some form of surveillance and control over him. In the nature of things the most recently conquered areas will be the furthest from the centre, and where communications are limited to the speed of a horse or even that of a fast runner, it will be over them that it is hardest to maintain authority.

On the furthest fringes vassal kingdoms and subject populations must have revolted and been reconquered, or brought to order by force when rebellion was threatened, more than once in a kingdom's history; and of course rebellions that could not be put down marked stages in the decline of empires. We hear, for example, of seven campaigns by kings of Rwanda against the Tutsi chief of Gisaka, and of Hutu populations in the north who were never effectively subdued until the king had the support of German troops. Eighteenth-century records of Asante refer to several expeditions for the reconquest of peoples who had earlier given their submission.

But what is more interesting is the way in which continuous relations were maintained between the dominant authority and populations with different degrees of autonomy. There was usually a central core in which the descendants of conquerors and conquered were together subject directly to the ruler through the medium of chiefs appointed by him. Where this is so, the criterion of distinction between core and periphery is the source of local authority—essentially, whether this is in the hands of bureaucrats or of subject rulers. From East Africa we learn more about the substitution of bureaucrats for lineage heads in the dominant population than we do about relations with tributary vassals; the history of the establishment of authority in Rwanda which was summarized earlier is one of the removal, not the control, of rival authorities. The least centralized kingdom that we know of is Ankole, despite the fact that it seems to have been expanding throughout the nineteenth century, when its authority over petty kingdoms whose relations with it were ambiguous was confirmed by the British government in Uganda. The periphery, as our sources describe it, consisted in the border areas of Ankole itself, where chiefs appointed from among the king's retainers were mainly responsible for defence, but had to rely largely on warrior cattle owners who had offered to the king an allegiance that they were able to withdraw if they felt strong enough to protect their own interests, or preferred to attach themselves to a neighbouring king.

The Core and the Periphery

It is, however, in West Africa that we are able to see clearly the distinction between core and periphery and the kind of relations maintained between superior rulers and their vassal states. Attached to the Habe kingdom of Zazzau (which has been called Zaria since the Fulani conquest that was launched in 1804) in the days of its independence were four small vassal states. The king of Zazzau had the formal right to appoint the rulers of these states, although there is no record of any interference with hereditary succession as this was understood by their own subjects. But a vassal on his succession had to be formally confirmed in office, either by an envoy of the king sent to receive his allegiance or by the king himself if he came to the capital to offer it. The king presented him with the insignia of office, of which, here as in so many places, the principal was a drum. He described himself as a client or dependent of the king, as some among his subjects would call themselves his own clients, and was required to pay tribute and supply soldiers when called upon.

The Fulani conquerors were themselves vassals of the Sultan of Sokoto, the direct descendant of the leader in the holy war, and were linked to him in much the same way. The Emir of Zaria was expected to visit Sokoto, taking the due tribute with him, at the two great annual Muslim festivals. The amount demanded was steadily increased, and by the end of the century an Emir was expected to make gifts in addition, on his own accession and on that of a Sultan. A third of an Emir's property went to the Sultan when he died. The Sultan claimed the right to dismiss the rulers of Zaria as well as to appoint them, and this right was exercised on a number of occasions. What made this burdensome allegiance worth while was that, from the time of the Fulani conquest, there was competition for the throne between the members of three lineages, in which the Sultan's support was an important factor. There is record of a rebellion of another vassal of Sokoto in 1850, when Zaria and three other Emirs sent troops for a campaign against him (which was unsuccessful). But on other occasions Zaria was entitled to ask for military aid from Sokoto.

The southward expansion of Fulani rule was effected not by combined forces directed from Sokoto but by the independent enterprise of those Fulani whose domains bordered on pagan lands. Thus Zaria itself added to the number of its vassals, and sometimes vassal states were exchanged between neighbouring Fulani kingdoms. Both in Habe Zazzau and in Fulani Sokoto a court official was responsible for dealings between each vassal and his overlord. Affairs in Zaria were in charge of the Sultan's senior official, the Wazir, who in time came to demand a separate tribute for himself when he visited the city once a year.

The Dahomean method of keeping the periphery in subjection was unusual. When a people were defeated in war, their villages were destroyed and the population driven away; if they came back they were attacked again. But if their king was killed the king of Dahomey appointed an official to replace him and allowed them to stay where they were or, if they had fled, to return to their homes.

The 'core' of the Asante empire consisted of Kumase with five states close to it (the 'five great peoples') which are said to have offered their allegiance to the conqueror Osei Tutu when he made it his capital. Hereditary succession to the headship of these states was and still is recognized, though the Asantehene, like the British in their 'indirect rule' territories, could remove individuals and could influence the succession. Superficially their position resembled that of subordinate chiefs anywhere; they levied tribute from their own subjects as well as that required by the Asantehene, they tried cases with an appeal to him. Just as the great Nyoro chiefs wore beaded crowns like the king's, they wore 'the little silver circles like buckles which distinguish the sandals of the king' (Bowdich, cited Wilks 1975: 113). But they and their descendants were always conscious that they had not received delegated authority from the Asantehene but had surrendered elements of their own power. The British consul Dupuis in 1820 thought the chief of Dwaben (who had been described as the Asantehene's 'brother king') was 'an independent ally', and was sharply rapped on the knuckles by the Asantehene for saying so; but it is just possible that the Dwabenhene thought the same. Mampon and Dwaben both went to war on their own, and at first at any rate levied their own tribute from the peoples they conquered; the Asantehene eventually took over Mampon's rights in payment of a debt owed him. These two states fought each other over their northern conquests, but the Asantehene asserted his right to settle the dispute, though nobody knows what the settlement was. In 1831 Dwaben had to be reduced by fighting. From the beginning there was a centrally controlled army in the sense that each of the five chiefs had a title designing the place of his contingent in it. Later, taxes of different kinds were levied directly on individuals and no longer in the form of tribute assessed on an area; this is referred to by several writers as 'exemption from tribute' and is taken by Wilks as a defining criterion of incorporation. Nevertheless, it can only have been because they preserved their sense of autonomy that all these chiefdoms toyed with the idea of secession after the defeat of Asante by the British in 1874.

Boundaries between the metropolitan region and the inner provinces, and between these and the outer, were marked by posts where travellers were stopped, might be refused passage, and had to pay dues, on each of·the 'great roads' that radiated outwards from Kumase. This in itself tells us little about any difference in political relations with Kumase between the inner and outer provinces. An ingenious calculation by Wilks, based on Asante statements about the number of days a journey to various different points was supposed to take, leads him to relate the effectiveness of control to 'message-delay'. He concludes that the minimum message-delay from Kumase—the time taken to send a message *and get an answer*—was six to twelve days in the metropolitan (the 'core') region, about a month in the inner provinces, and up to seven weeks in the outer provinces to the north. In this connection he remarks that messages had to be memorized by their carriers. But early in the nineteenth century written documents, carried in boxes, were becoming common.

The distinction made by the nineteenth-century writers between subjects and tributaries corresponds to that made elsewhere in this chapter between subjects and vassals. Although Dupuis wrote of the 'tributaries' as being 'left to the government of their own caboceers' (cited Wilks 1975: 63), this hardly seems to be a crucial distinction when we recall that even the five 'great peoples' had their own chiefs. What is more significant is that in the more distant provinces an emissary from the metropolis resided permanently. These men were nominated by the great chiefs of the Asantehene, who here, as in Zazzau, were each made responsible for certain of the outlying areas.

Nadel (1942), writing of the Emirate of Nupe, describes a very much more fluid situation, one in which the core was hardly more effectively controlled than the periphery. Within the kingdom proper the princes and other office-holders fought among themselves or raided 'outer peoples' who, having paid the tribute due from them in slaves, had a claim to be left in peace. Moreover, the Emir might countenance raids on these 'protected persons'; all they were in fact protected against was raids from other states. Nadel refers to chiefs 'put in charge' of these districts, but his not very clear statements seem to imply that the sole 'charge' was the responsibility to go with an army to collect the tribute.

The principle followed in Dahomey, that conquered peoples were not allowed to return to their homes unless they surrendered the head of their king, was hardly compatible with the recognition of tributary vassals. According to Le Hérissé (cited Argyle 1966: 29–30), after the conquest of the related kingdom of Allada the king's chief minister was made responsible for it, but he did not have to go and live there. We are also told, however, that Dahomean kings sometimes appointed heads of conquered towns from among the population and sometimes from among their own followers.

Territorial Authority

While these differences in modes of controlling peripheral populations are interesting, the possibilities of greatest elaboration are to be found in the government of the people who are held to be directly subject to the king. The simplest way of delegating authority within such a realm would be to carve it up (notionally) into a number of geographical areas, each with a single head responsible to the king for law and order, and for the organization of whatever services and payments were required. This was what the kingdoms in Uganda looked like when they had been streamlined by British authorities who were supposedly maintaining the traditional system with just a little tidying up. It is, apparently, what Asante really was like, since all its states kept their traditional boundaries and the Asantehene's sanctions against their hereditary rulers took the form of fines. But in many places, kings were constantly creating new chiefdoms to reward their followers, and these could not always be found in newly conquered territory. In Buganda it is recorded that the twenty-second Kabaka created a new kind of chiefdom called *butongole*, by placing loyal followers whom he wished to reward in authority over sections of the wider areas that have commonly been called counties in English. These posts were not hereditary, so that it was not absolutely necessary to keep founding new ones, but their numbers did continually increase. The holders were subject to the general authority of the county chiefs, but were clearly in a different relation to them from that of the subordinates whom they chose themselves. They raised troops from the areas under their control, but these were not part of the county chief's contingent; they led their men directly to the capital. Father Gorju, writing in 1920, compared them to a parasitic organism attached to the county chief; their direct relation to the Kabaka implied the obligation of spying on other authorities and was one way of restricting the power of the greater territorial chiefs, as was the appointment of paired chiefs in Rwanda. Estates allotted to queen-mothers were under the authority of chiefs, who may perhaps have been included among the *baton-gole*. Others again supplied revenues for chiefs with duties at court. In addition, in the nineteenth century further areas were given to the military chiefs who were mentioned in Chapter II.

There was a recognized rank order among the ten great chiefs, but there was no 'promotion ladder' such as existed in some West African kingdoms. Nor could there have been as long as it was possible for them to maintain a claim to hereditary office, and the kings who refused in the nineteenth century to recognize such claims were not likely to tie themselves to any other formula that would limit their freedom of choice.

In some kingdoms even major chiefs were not given authority over large contiguous areas. Bradbury describes the divisions of Benin as 'tribute units', villages or groups of villages from which various individuals were responsible for collecting tribute and providing manpower for public works or war; most of these went with chiefly titles, though they could be transferred from one title to another, and the areas under any one title might be scattered all over the kingdom. Similarly in Fulani Zazzau the 'tribute units', or 'fiefs' as M. G. Smith prefers to call them, consisted of numbers of small towns with the hamlets attached to them. Each of these had its own head, a member of the local community, and the actual execution of orders from above was in this man's hands. A large fief-holder would have agents in charge of different parts of his estates, and he could appoint and transfer them at will. They were his clients as he and the other fief-holders were clients of the king, and for both categories a title was the evidence of right to authority. Some titles in Zazzau were claimed as hereditary, but in the main the king disposed of them as he pleased, and in Smith's view transferred or demoted the holders less in the interests of efficiency than in that of rewarding his followers; this fact is connected with the rule that the kingship rotated between lineages, each of which did its best for its own members.

As Gluckman describes the organization of Barotseland it

was individuals who were set under the authority of different titles, and when a new title was created its holder was given resources and responsibilities by attaching to it 'people scattered over Barotseland'. Such a division of the population was called a *likolo*, a word which Gluckman translates as 'sector'. The chief of any sector had subordinates, among whom the sector members were not necessarily distributed individually; people could 'take affairs' (1951: 33) to any chief of their sector, but whatever these affairs were, in judicial matters they went to the capital, where all the chiefs of the sector held court as a body. People were summoned by sectors for public works, or war, or for large communal hunts. Only on the periphery of the kingdom were non-Lozi populations sometimes attached *en bloc* to one sector, and even there this was not done systematically. For purposes of tribute payment there was yet another arrangement; people were allocated, again as individuals, to a number of 'storehouses' for which 'stewards' were responsible. How this system could have been maintained over the generations in a society which did not recognize unilineal descent groups it is very hard to see, and Gluckman only tells us that it was 'extremely difficult to work out the framework of this very complicated administrative system', but that every Lozi knew exactly where he fitted into it (1951: 39). But however the system came into being, it had the same result as the less complicated one in Benin, that there were no territorially based political units of a size to constitute a threat to the royal authority; and it was valued by the Barotse people, who were indignant when it was destroyed by British authorities in the interests of efficiency. The councillors who agreed to the change, Gluckman tells us, writing shortly after the event, 'have been discharged by the whole nation'. How? That he does not tell us.

The practical need to distribute authority over divisions of a kingdom is obvious; in addition this distribution could sometimes solve the problem of satisfying (or neutralizing) the ambitions of members of royal lineages. In such kingdoms as that of the Azande or the Luba princes this problem was solved by territorial expansion, a process that went on until fixed boundaries were imposed under colonial rule. In the

Interlacustrine Bantu kingdoms princes were kept under strict control, occasionally massacred lest they attack their royal brothers. In Asante sons of kings, who in this matrilineal society had no direct claim to the kingship, were often appointed to bureaucratic positions; rivalry between members of the royal lineage seems to have been confined to competition for the succession. In Benin during the period of its expansion members of the royal lineage, usually the sons of the king's brother, were given an authority over outlying districts which was then recognized to be hereditary; they did not displace the village heads who held their position by right of seniority but exercised varying degrees of control over them. The implications of the Zaria rule of rotating succession have been mentioned, and will be discussed again in connection with various types of political competition.

If the need to create subordinate authorities offered kings a way of rewarding their supporters and endowing their kin, the need to reward supporters and endow kinsmen could lead to the proliferation of offices. The most remarkable example of this is the system which developed in Lesotho after the kingdom became a British colony. As a colony Lesotho (then Basutoland) had fixed frontiers and a rapidly expanding population, not least among the royal lineage with its many wives. British authority there for a long time was confined to supporting the king (now Paramount Chief) and maintaining order; it did not seek, as elsewhere, to reorganize the administrative system until as late as 1938.

Out of the very common idea that princes should be set in authority over outlying districts, and the by no means uncommon idea that the heir to a chiefdom or kingdom should serve an apprenticeship in administration, there evolved the practice of 'placing' not only all the king's many sons but those of the senior chiefs (themselves descended from him) in authority over areas from which they derived revenues, and a belief on the part of these royal sons that they had a claim to be maintained in this way. When a chief's son was 'placed' the existing chief was not dismissed but became his subordinate, with the legal consequence that cases tried by him could be appealed to the newcomer. Only the humble headmen or village chiefs who were originally members of the small local community were eventually crowded out by royal kin, so that the number of chiefs continually increased.

When a royal son was 'placed' he traditionally built his own village, the land for which had to be provided by the chief already in authority over the area. The latter was asked to designate the 'place', but in practice he might find he had to give up half his domain, and within this area the new chief could himself 'place' kinsmen and followers. Then he would begin to require the chief who had been demoted to make room for him to provide him with services—ploughing and gathering firewood, the latter a service customarily demanded by Sotho chiefs. In a case recorded by Ashton (1952: 201–2) the earlier chief ultimately lost one-third of his subjects. Boundaries were not clearly drawn, except in cases where disputes were referred to magistrate's courts, and the new chief would be constantly trying to extend the area under his direct control. Where both the senior chief and his subordinate had sons to 'place' there was even more competition.

A report made in 1935 on the administration of Basutoland was highly critical of a system under which chiefs could be said (by one of their subjects) to be 'as many as there are stars in the heavens', and shortly afterwards the British authorities decided to cut down the number whose authority they would recognize. Such a policy, though clearly desirable for administrative efficiency, only increased the anxieties of the lower level chiefs whose position was already insecure. At the time when it was being implemented there was an outbreak of murders committed in order to use the victim's flesh for magical purposes, and some of these were undoubtedly organized by chiefs who thought that to have such medicines would strengthen their position.

Specialist offices: Asante

The more complex the organization of the kingdom, the more necessary it was to create specialized offices concerned with particular aspects of national business. As was indicated in the previous chapter, specialized military officials can sometimes be found in kingdoms where other special responsibilities are confined to the upkeep of the palace and the control of its population. Other specialist officers were generally based on the capital, and if they were in charge of activities outside they might nominate henchmen to represent them on the spot. But a striking exception is to be found in connection with the control of trade in those West African kingdoms that depended on it. We learn how this was managed from the records of traders which go back to the seventeenth century.

Bosman wrote in 1700 of Dahomey: 'For every Affair that can be thought of the King hath appointed a Captain Overseer, also a great many Honorary Captains'. He specified as the Grand Captains, whom he also called Vice-Roys, the Captain of the Market, the Captain of Slaves, the Captain of the Tron (prison), and the Captain of the Shore; though he did not describe the duties of the last-named, he must have been in charge of transactions with the trading ships, as were two of the Benin palace officials. Later the four Vice-Roys were described as being responsible for dealing respectively with Portuguese, English, French, and Dutch ships. They or their servants watched the landing of goods, and before anyone else could buy, they agreed the amount to be paid in customs, and then bought on the king's behalf such goods as he required, notably fire-arms and powder, over which he maintained a strict control; often he pre-empted as much as two-thirds of the cargo. Sellers of slaves were required to pay a tax on each man sold. Canoe trading by African middlemen was supervised in the same way.

As the organization of a kingdom becomes more complex, it can be expected that new needs will be met by assigning additional responsibilities to existing palace officials. This is what happened in the creation of the Asante king's company of traders. Its original members were the king's drummers and horn-blowers, men whose duties in the palace were not strictly limited to what was implicit in their designation. An Asante told Wilks that they 'did any job which the Asantehene required'. They accompanied the singers who on state occasions chanted the names of royal ancestors, and the horn-blowers every midnight played a sort of national anthem which, so Bowdich was told, represented the king's thanks to his officers and people. But both they and the drummers also kept the palace in repair and were responsible for royal burials. Their leading members, like the Ganda royal cooks and butchers, were important persons. As early as 1714 a 'King of Ashantee's Drummer' was visiting the coast to buy guns. As Asante trade increased and the king imposed strict control upon it, the chief of the horn-blowers became the head of the traders, a 'company' or 'department' called the *batafo*. The leading men of this company received advances in gold dust from the Asantehene with which they bought their trading stock, or, alternatively, paid for the guns and powder that they bought from the coast. The gold-dust was given out at the Adae ceremonies which were held every six weeks, and when an expedition came back, its leader gave an account (both financial and narrative) of its activities and a share of the profit made was allotted to the members of the expedition. The Asokwahene, the hereditary head of the company, an office that went with authority over territory near Kumase, nominated the leaders of different expeditions, and they collected carriers from the villages under his control, some of these being slaves and some women; there would also be an armed guard. A caravan might number two or three hundred people.

A participant's account of such an expedition was given to Rattray by an old man who described the typical organization. It is worth noting that he was talking of a caravan sent out not by the Asantehene himself but by the chief of Mampon, since this shows that the bands of functionaries at a subordinate court closely paralleled those of Kumase. This old man recalled an annual journey to the north to sell kola nuts, the one stimulant permitted to Moslims, for which the demand rose steeply after the re-establishment of orthodox Islam in the northern kingdoms by the Fulani conquest. The kola nuts were bought in the forests between Mampon and Kumase. The caravan would leave early in the season when prices were high, accompanied by messengers whose golden-hilted state swords showed that they were official emissaries, and, when it had passed, the same messengers closed the road to other travellers to prevent competition by private traders. When they had done their business the road was opened, and a toll, in nuts, not in gold-dust, was collected from any other traders who passed; one-fifth of this was kept by the collectors. The official traders were allowed to deal on their own account in small quantities of nuts in addition to the loads carried on behalf of the chief, which were of a standard size, 1,500 or 2,000 nuts. These expeditions may have had slaves with them carrying food, but Rattray's informant said 'it was no disgrace for a free man to carry a load while trading' (Rattray 1929: 109–111).

The royal revenues in gold-dust were in charge of a special company under the Gyaasewahene. The total reserves were kept in one enormous box, and according to tradition it was held to be desirable that this should be full. Wilks (1975: 419) calculated that it could hold gold dust to the value of £1,500,000 sterling at nineteenth-century rates. Its contents were kept in reserve, while wooden boxes and glass flagons were used for smaller, but nevertheless appreciable, amounts. Each held 1,000 peredwans (about £8,000), and each peredwan was separately wrapped in cloth, as were smaller quantities. It would be from these that the Asantehene made his advances to traders at the Adae. Goldsmiths (another company) worked in a room next to that in which the great chest was kept, reducing the nuggets to dust. Around 1870 about 100 men were employed in this work. Gold-dust was weighed when it was received or paid out; this was the responsibility of another company, the 'openers of the bag'; the bag, an elaborate decorated leather satchel with a padlock, was a container not of money but of implements for weighing. A rough account was kept by the simple method of putting a cowrie shell in the box whenever a peredwan was taken out, and removing one each time this amount was paid in. As Rattray points out, the people concerned in money transactions remembered them with remarkable accuracy, as those who have to get on without written records often do.

Two companies of officials were concerned with road communications. The *akwanmofo* were created in the eighteenth century 'for cleaning the roads and paths of the kingdom of nuisances', that is seeing that the authorities through whose land they passed kept them open. They had funds to pay for the work and were authorized to fine those 'committing a nuisance'—Reindorf's phrase, which Wilks interprets as 'failing to keep the ways cleared'. Just as collectors of tribute or other dues (of which there were many) were remunerated by keeping a share of what they collected, so the road inspectors were entitled to a share of these fines.

The *nkwansrafo* (police) lived permanently at points on the great roads—the points, says Wilks (1975: 48), where they crossed the boundaries of the metropolitan region. If the metropolitan region is defined as the area entry into which is subject to control, this description is a tautology. However, the fact is that travellers who arrived at these posts were stopped and questioned, and not allowed to go further until a messenger had gone to the capital and come back with permission. It was the *nkwansrafo* who collected the tolls, and who closed the roads to individuals who might seek to compete with the official traders. At one time there were reported to be 500 or 600 armed men at one of these posts.

Along with the 'sword-bearers', whose presence guaranteed the official character of any mission, for trading or simply to convey messages, there were heralds (who sometimes seem to have been the same people) and 'criers'. According to Rattray the main function of the heralds was at court, where they would intersperse the speech of an important person with calls of 'Listen, listen' (something that was still being done to my knowledge in 1952), while the 'criers' went round the city beating the 'gong-gong', actually a not very resonant piece of metal struck with another piece of metal, to call attention to some announcement made from the court. Every chief had his own heralds and gong-beaters. Sometimes, it seems, they were sent all over the country to announce decisions if important.

Estimates were made from time to time of the numbers engaged in these different activities. The Gyaasewahene was said to have more than 1,000 men under him, and the company of heralds and gong-beaters to number 1,000. The 'official carriers'—of persons, not goods—numbered, in contrast, only 100. A senior official was entitled to build an open-fronted room (*dampan*) facing the public way in which he received people with requests to make, also to have a large decorated umbrella. European observers often counted the numbers of such umbrellas at meetings which they attended. Wilks (1975: 467) reckons that there were about 250 such notables, but these would include territorial as well as specialist authorities.

Although these bodies of men were called companies, they had little in common with the Benin associations. Theoretically appointment to posts of authority within them was in the gift of the Asantehene, but in practice they seem to have frequently passed from father to son. The general rule of succession in Asante was matrilineal, but a specialist official was expected to train his successor; if he chose a younger brother he would still be following the matrilineal rule, but it seems that when a set of brothers had been exhausted the next to succeed would be a son, not a sister's son, of his predecessor. As Wilks observes, the reason was that a post to which nomination was theoretically free would most likely be filled by someone who had acquired the necessary qualifications, and he again would most likely be one who had grown up in an official's household; but it is still not clear why these officials did not have sisters and their children living with them in the normal Asante family pattern. It is interesting too that when, under colonial rule, the titles describing the posts became purely honorific, they began to be inherited in the female line.

Highest of all in the state, after the king, were the men who have been called 'linguists' almost ever since anyone began to write about them in English. Rattray, the first anthropologist to write of Asante, called them 'spokesmen', a translation of their Twi name which more effectively indicates their functions. The *akyeame* spoke in the name of the king on public occasions, notably on the installation of chiefs and in trying court cases. It was also the *akyeame* who were the intermediaries between the Asantehene and subordinate chiefs (see Chapter III). A story recorded by Rattray (1929: 150) illustrates this duty. After the destruction of Kumase by Sir Garnet Wolseley in 1874 there was a general move to throw off the Asantehene's authority. Dwaben rebelled, and there seemed a danger that it would be joined by Bekwae. An *okyeame* and a sword-bearer were sent to summon the Bekwaehene to Kumase, where he asserted his loyalty and offered to commit his forces in action against Dwaben (a version which suggests that divisional chiefs did not automatically obey the royal order). But the king did not allow him to command his own troops for fear he should go over to Dwaben. When such a rebellion was successfully put down, it was for the *okyeame* to fix the indemnity to be paid. Every chief at whatever level had his *okyeame*. Those of the chiefs of the important companies were apparently appointed by the king, and they exercised as much influence on their activities as the chiefs themselves.

Specialist offices: Zazzau

The organization of the kingdom of Zazzau may well have been as complex as that of Asante, though the records of it that exist do not allow one to describe it in anything like the same detail. Here the senior official was a man promoted from among the palace eunuchs, who were recruited from a limited number of villages. This officer, the Galadima, held ultimate responsibility for all civil matters, including control over the territorial authorities. He was concerned with the maintenance of roads and ferries, with supplies to the capital, and in time of war to the army. He controlled the police, who were drawn from the king's slaves, and offenders who were tried in the capital were punished in his compound. In time of war the king went with the army and the Galadima acted as his deputy. Next to him came the military leader, the Madawaki, whose title means 'owner of the horses'. He too was appointed by promotion from the household officials, but as a free subject of the king he was rewarded for his services by the grant of fiefs, as well as the right to distribute among his own followers half of the spoils of any victorious campaign. Eunuch officials had no such right; they received a share of the taxes that they collected and were maintained as members of the royal household. Each of these two officials had territorial control over one half of the capital.

Next in rank to the Galadima were two other eunuchs, Wombai and Dallatu. The latter took the place of the Galadima on campaigns and was in charge of the army's 'civil administration' (i.e. commissariat?) (Smith 1960: 45). The Wombai is simple described as an assistant of the Galadima. Slaves were employed in other public duties, unspecified, as well as that of police, and titles were conferred on those holding authority in the different spheres. Collectively they were subject to the joint control of a subordinate of the Madawaki and of the head of the palace officials.

In the Hausa kingdom the mallams, the Koranic scholars, had purely religious functions, and should not be mentioned in a discussion of administrative organization but for the fact that a mallam could be appointed to a civil office, in which case he had to give up his priestly duties and his claim to be supported by alms.

The Fulani conquerors preserved certain elements of the traditional system, but with as much distortion as the British were later to make in their attempts to preserve such systems while adapting them to new requirements. In this case they had the initial advantage that most of the high officials of Zazzau fled with their king to Abuja.

In Habe Zazzau only three titles were held by members of the royal family, two of these being women. The third was the Dan Galadima, the king's chosen successor, who does not appear to have had any administrative responsibilities. Under the Fulani three lineages in turn were entitled to provide the ruler, an arrangement made by the Sultan of Sokoto to reward those who had taken major parts in the conquest. There was no strict order of succession, but it became the rule, a very rational one, that only a man who had held one of the senior titled offices could become king. Moreover the arrangement for the rotation of lineages implied that there were spoils of office of which each in turn should have its share. The king was now expected to appoint to 'offices of profit' one son of each of his wives, and in addition to find posts for other kinsmen and affines. The highest offices were considered to be appropriate for sons, others for grandsons, of a king; the latter category could not succeed. No longer were the highest offices rendered politically neutral by reserving them for men who could have no heirs; now they were key positions in struggles for power.

A comparison of the Fulani system with that which preceded it seems to indicate that there were fewer organizations directly dependent on high officials at the capital, and that instead all holders of territorial authority were general purpose officers.

They still lived at the capital, leaving subordinates in actual charge of their districts, which were in practice allotted as fiefs to persons whom the king wished to reward or favour. Some of these fiefs came in practice to be hereditary; others were re-allocated during the lifetime of the holders. The fief-holder had the ultimate responsibility for the basic requirements of political peace and the observance of Islamic law, for the collection of tribute and labour and the provision of manpower for civil and military purposes. The essential difference between African kingdoms in this respect was in the nature of the public works required. At the minimum what was called for was the maintenance of the residences of kings and chiefs; then the clearing of roads, something in which Buganda was exceptional in East Africa but which was normal in the west. Fulani Zazzau was concerned with the upkeep of town walls, mosques, and markets, the last item implying law and order as well as clearing weeds.

A major innovation made by the Fulani was to entrust judicial functions to the mallams as part of the restoration of the strict law of Islam which had been the motive of their crusade. Such a recognition of professional judges might be thought to imply that separation of powers which western nations have considered vital to civil liberties. The mallams were entitled to try officials for an offence called *zalunci* or maladministration, which is condemned by the authoritative exponents of Islam. But whereas the word had originally implied oppressive rule, it came to mean no more than failure to carry out the ruler's orders.

Slaves

Missing from the list of services that a fief-holder could claim is one that is conspicuous in all accounts from other regions of Africa: farm work as a contribution to the food supply of a king's or chief's capital. The reason lies in the major contrast between the west and the other regions, its reliance for manpower on slaves. Not that war captives were not made servants elsewhere, but they were attached to the households of their captors and little differentiated from the rest, except that the most disagreeable work would fall to them. But in West Africa

slaves were an object of wealth; rulers demanded them in tribute, Africans as well as Europeans bought them for whatever
was accepted as currency in different areas. One of the tenets of
Islam was that the faithful were entitled to enslave the infidels,
and in Zaria raiding for slaves in the non-Islamic subject areas
did not count as war or require royal permission.

Thus the slaves of an important man were far too numerous
to be treated as household dependents; they were a labour force
which freed him from the necessity of directly providing his
own subsistence; they were capital just as machinery is capital.
Both in Zaria and in Benin slaves were settled in villages where
they cultivated land for their masters, and in Benin they cultivated oil palms as an export crop. In Zaria the members of
the three royal lineages were entitled to create separate slave
villages and even sometimes small walled towns, which came
under their direct authority and on which they paid no tax or
tribute. But others, and everyone in Benin, had to get authorization—in effect, the right to occupy land—from territorial
authorities before setting up such villages, and in Benin there
might be bands of slaves of different masters in the same village.

Of Asante Bowdich wrote that slaves were employed 'to
create plantations in the more remote and stubborn tracts'
(cited Wilks 1975: 52), though when he wrote of Kumase he
said these remote parts were only two or three miles from the
town; there, the slaves produced the food for their masters'
large households in the town and also 'fruit and vegetables for
sale', and looked after some of their masters' numerous children. A significant occupation for slaves was gold-mining, the
very basis of the economy of the kingdom. The Asante held this
to be a profanation of the earth for which they themselves, if
they picked up gold, would suffer ritual punishment.

CHAPTER VII

THE RESOURCES OF KINGDOMS

Reciprocity or Exploitation?

DURING the period between the establishment and the withdrawal of European rule in Africa the attitudes of the thinking people among the ruling nations towards the political institutions of the subject ones went through a series of changes, and we see yet a new phase in the interpretation of those institutions now that it is for Africans themselves to judge how far they deserve to be maintained.

However much the expansion of Europe in Africa was dictated by material interests, some of the individuals who took part in it had other aims—the dissemination of Christian belief and with it of the values then held to be associated with 'civilization'. Of course it was reassuring for those who were seeking their fortunes to be told that this was an incidental part of the process, but they were not much concerned with details of the ways in which African institutions fell short of the civilized ideal. It was those responsible for the administration of African territories who thought it was their duty to introduce just rule and free Africans from oppression, an attitude which led them to interpret African rule in terms of injustice and oppression: Africans must be freed from arbitrary exactions in the economic sphere, arbitrary decisions in the political. In some places this led to the total suppression of African authority, in others—those from which most of the material in this book is taken—to attempts to improve standards of African rule.

A revulsion accompanied the recognition that European rule had been by no means wholly just nor self-denying in the field of exactions. This did not in itself lead to a revaluation of African rule, but it was associated, for those who wanted to know what African institutions were really like, with the functional theory of anthropology which asserted that the institutions that non-industrial peoples had developed for themselves were those best suited to their needs, and should not be arbitrarily modified by paternalist outsiders. At the same time some administrative officers were looking at the people for whom they were responsible with eyes that saw something other than abuses to be suppressed. Anthropologists began to talk in terms of reciprocity, the return that a king made to his subjects for the prestations that he demanded of them, and of consensus, the reasons that led them to accept his rule as legitimate. An element in their attitude was that they conceived it as their duty to present the institutions of the societies they studied without the adverse prejudices that were and still are widely current among the uninformed; and at the very least they were prepared to maintain that those institutions were valued by the people whose lives they regulated.

More recently a new trend has appeared, which is associated with the popularity of new interpretations of Marxism, though not all the writers who follow it would call themselves Marxists. In this interpretation, traditional African political systems are again represented as exploitative and oppressive and as resting on coercion rather than consensus; and this of course is consistent with the view that all political authority is so. This is the attitude at present of only a minority of anthropologists. But these alternative interpretations need to be examined.

Since the economic functions of government are essential to its organization, we should consider first the question whether the taxpayers and tributaries in African kingdoms thought they got, or did get, an adequate or fair return for their contribution to the upkeep of the kingdom. Where peripheral vassal states are concerned, it might sometimes be difficult to argue that they did. Yet Bowdich was quite clear about what was gained by Dagomba as tributary of Asante: 'at the expense of an inconsiderable tribute he established a commercial intercourse which, his markets being regularly supplied from the interior, was both an advantage and a security to him' (Bowdich 1819: 234, cited Goody 1968: 203). And when Asante authority was rejected after 1874, the prosperity of the trading cities declined. By that time, evidently, Dagomba made the calculation differ-

ently. To outsiders attempting objective assessment, the bene-
fits of security would seem clearly greater where trade was
more important.

On the whole it is from small kingdoms or from the core
areas of empires that we can sometimes learn how subjects
envisaged the nature of their exchange with their rulers.
Sometimes this was an exchange of material for intangible
goods; taxes maintain the authorities, certainly at a somewhat
higher level than the majority of their subjects, though this
depends to some extent on the total resources of the kingdom,
and in return they receive institutions for the settlement of
disputed claims which make it unnecessary to seek private
redress. There is evidence that the law-enforcing function of
authority is valued. The neighbours of the Alur, chiefdoms so
tiny that they have not been discussed in this book, would ask
an Alur chief to send them one of his sons, who, they thought,
had the necessary hereditary ritual power, to live among them
and settle their disputes. Cynics have argued that traditions of
such incidents are merely inventions to justify Alur expansion.
But Elizabeth Colson, writing of the acephalous Tonga of
Zambia, is satisfied that they welcomed the coming of an over-
riding authority (in this case British) which made it unnecessary for them to rely on force to settle their quarrels. What they
valued was not so much, or not only, greater security, but a
method of decision that was more expeditious than the gathering of kin and friends, perhaps from a distance, to support one's
case in a discussion among equals. She cites other societies
which abandoned the pursuit of claims by force as soon as they
heard of the coming of administrative courts 'almost as if they
had only been waiting an excuse to give it up' (Sorrenson 1972,
cited Colson 1974: 65). Jacob Black-Michaud, writing of
Albania, where feuds were carried on till a later period than
anywhere else in Europe, notes that they repeatedly told
enquirers that 'what they really needed ... was a strong
government with an efficient army to compel them to abandon
the feud' (1975: 134). Of course everyone believes that unfair
judgements are given in individual cases, particularly cases that
he has lost himself, but this does not contradict the view that
judicial institutions in themselves are valued.

The second question to be asked is that of the economic returns for the tribute and services given. The Azande were very clear on this. *Ru ae*, gifts to a prince, should, they said, be balanced by *fu ae*, gifts to his subjects. 'If raw beans went into the royal residence they ought to return to court as cooked beans; if termite oil went into the royal residence it ought to return to court as a relish to flavour porridge; if malted eleusine went into the royal residence it ought to return to the inner court as brewed beer; and if the subjects cultivated their masters' eleusine, the harvest ought to be pounded, ground, and cooked as porridge for those same subjects to eat at court'. 'It was fully understood on both sides that labour and tribute were for this purpose' (Evans-Pritchard 1971: 215).

Bowdich described the distribution of food at the Asante court in 1819, where a peredwan of gold (£8 at the rate of the time) was spent daily on palm wine served to 'the retinue of all captains attending'; an element of royal ceremonial was the appearance of the king in public to drink with his people. Sometimes brass pans containing rum were carried through the street for the populace to drink. Here one can see the contrast between the circulation of commodities within a small population, those in attendance at a Zande court, and in one as great and as widely spread on the ground as that of Asante, where clearly a much smaller proportion got this sort of return for what they gave. But later writers on Asante, both British and African, emphasize the public purposes on which the royal revenues were expended.

Another kind of argument for the legitimacy of tribute is that summarized by Basil Sansom (1974: 148) as characteristic of the southern Bantu in general. 'The logic of tribute is that it is sent as "thanks" to an administrator for doing work to make production of the commodity represented possible.' He is referring to the function of a chief or headman in allocating land for production, in co-ordinating productive activities and perhaps also in performing ritual for propitious weather. This reverses the commoner description of this kind of reciprocity—he collects tribute but is expected to return it—in a very interesting way.

According to the recently published recollections of an old

Sotho, the subjects of Moshweshwe's successors had a clear idea
of the services that could and could not legitimately be asked of
them. A chief had three 'lands', the produce of one of which
was reckoned to supply provisions for the army, while the other
two were for his personal needs. His subjects were called on to
plough these, and were not rewarded with beer or a meat feast
as was common elsewhere. 'But they were pleased to do it; they
knew they were cultivating their own land.' Jingoes recalls an
occasion when a work-party finished the ploughing early in the
day and were asked to plough two private lands of the chief's
wives. They agreed as a favour, but when he wanted them to
do still more work, they refused. 'Where does the food from
these fields go? Not to us! Do you think we are going to work in
your mothers' lands without getting food for our work?'
(Jingoes 1975: 174–5).

The extreme opposite evaluation of the relation between
tribute and return is that made by Jaques Maquet (1961) in his
study of Rwanda. Certainly we are dealing here with a ruling
and a subject population, and it could be argued—he would
perhaps argue himself—that the whole Hutu population stood
in the same relation to the ruling Tutsi as the tribute-paying
vassals did in the more extensive empires, getting nothing back
except protection from rival exploiters.

The sources of tribute in Rwanda were those typical of the
Bantu kingdoms. A proportion of their cattle was taken from
Tutsi, and vegetable food was collected at harvest from Hutu.
Only Hutu were called upon for labour. Maquet calculates
that the amount required was equivalent to one third of the
time of one member of an extended family; all recent accounts
say that the labour demand, though not the tribute in kind,
was resented. As Maquet interprets the function of tribute, it
was solely to 'provide the ruling class with consumption goods'
(1961: 104), and to maintain it in power. The share of tribute
retained by the collectors was no more than a reward for their
loyalty to the king, and the services rendered by government,
which to so many anthropologists, and, as my quotations
indicate, to some Africans, have seemed to be identical with
those that are the basic functions of any state, were nothing of
the kind. They were legitimized not by the ideology of reci-

procity but by that of divine right. Exactions, Maquet argues, were pushed to the limit beyond which the subjects would have either starved or moved to the realm of another ruler, a cynical inversion of the argument that a check on oppressive government was the need to conciliate followers who would otherwise transfer their allegiance. If the political system did provide a minimum of security from physical violence, this was merely incidental.

Oberg (1961), without going quite so far, says that the Hima (the Nkole counterparts of the Tutsi) 'endeavoured to keep [the Iru] in subjection' so as to be able to count on tribute from them. Herdsmen visiting the royal court expected to be fed on porridge all the time they were there. Some Iru craftsmen—makers of spears and milk pots—were attached to every chief as his servants (but presumably at least partially maintained by him), and some of the objects they made were distributed to Hima visiting the chief, a practice which, according to Oberg, limited the amount of free barter open to the Iru.

Naturally the most elaborate ways of obtaining resources for the state are to be found where total resources are greater, and products and occupations more varied. In the West African kingdoms there were far greater differences of wealth and poverty, and many of the wealthy—though not all—were holders of office who took their share of tax and tribute. If their economies are described as redistributive it is because every dignitary had his own retinue who received some reward for his services, some of them perhaps getting their whole subsistence. It is in this sense that the state was the largest employer, as indeed it is in many parts of independent Africa today. Behind the rational calculations of the balance of advantage which taxpayers must surely have made, there lay, of course, usually in some form an ideology supporting the claims of the king himself, of the sacredness of kingship carrying with it the belief in ritual sanctions against disobedience, though certainly these were never wholly effective. As a justification for the claim on the subjects' property this might be put in the form given to Herskovits (admittedly long after Dahomey had ceased to be a kingdom): 'If the king is fed Dahomey will not fail to prosper' (cited Argyle 1966: 102).

Writers on West Africa make a distinction which is not found in the literature on the Bantu, between tax and tribute. For them a tribute is a lump sum demanded from a subject area, a tax a payment levied on individuals, and nineteenth-century observers in Asante distinguished on this basis between subjects and tributary provinces of the empire. When the imperial power began to weaken after 1874, the states which broke away resented both the tribute which had been collected by force, with the destruction of villages if they failed to pay it, and also the demand for contingents of troops. Perhaps all this meant was that former tributary chiefs now kept for themselves all that they collected.

Revenues in Dahomey

From the point of view of organization, however, the interest lies in the kind of activity for which, or circumstances in which, a tax was held to be due. European traders were naturally most concerned with dues and tolls on trade, and so have described how they were collected; some aspects of this were anticipated in the discussion of types of state servant. These traders paid a customs duty before buying and selling could begin. Benin records do not tell us much of this process, but many of those who wrote on the Slave Coast, before and during the time when the port of Whydah was subject to Dahomey, have left descriptions of what happened. First the merchant stated what he had to sell and what he wanted to buy. In Dahomey, before the trade was suppressed, slaves were the only commodity; later the only export was palm-oil. Samples of the goods brought were chosen, and were sent to the king by a messenger bearing a staff marked with the emblem of the company offering them. The prices were fixed by bargaining. Then the customs due were paid in goods, the amount being calculated, as late as 1870, not on the quantity of goods or even on the tonnage of the ships but on the number of their masts (Skertchly 1874: 22). In addition a large portion of the cargo was bought by the king before any could be sold elsewhere, and his slaves were sold at a higher price, either in cowrie currency or in goods, than those of his subjects. Also the traders had to buy as many slaves as he wished to sell before they could deal with anyone else. In addition he collected from his subjects a gun and gunpowder from every slave they sold, and those who bought liquor from the European fort paid a proportion which was measured out in a coconut shell (this information comes from Le Hérissé, a French official writing in 1911; it is not easy to see how this tax in kind could have been transported, but perhaps it was part of the tax-gatherer's payment).

Like Asante, Dahomey collected tolls from traders passing certain posts. Those of Dahomey had a fence across the path with only a narrow space to go through, which could be easily closed. Bosman said the king had 'above one thousand collectors, who disperse themselves throughout the whole land ... There is nothing so mean sold in the whole kingdom, that the King hath not toll for it.' The toll-houses on the roads are thought to have been taken over from the petty states that Dahomey absorbed; they had political as well as economic functions, in that everyone passing through had to swear that he planned no evil against the king. No doubt because the subjection of the coastal peoples was always in question, the control kept over their movements was even stricter than it was in Asante; every company of travellers carried a 'passport', which was either a bundle of pebbles equal in numbers to that of its members or a notched stick. Skertchly, travelling with a royal escort which was exempt from scrutiny, noticed as he left Whydah that his retinue had become unexpectedly large. The tolls were not heavy; the collectors kept a small proportion as their reward and had the rest carried, by slaves or hired porters, to the superior chiefs to whom they were assigned. Tolls were also collected at the local markets where foodstuffs, drink, pots, and magical substances, and even water, were sold; the proceeds are said to have gone to the upkeep of the royal tombs.

Every individual, including children old enough to run messages, was liable for a payment the name for which Le Hérissé translates as 'sleep money' (payment for existing?), and this was first imposed in order to buy guns from the coastal traders. A most elaborate census procedure for calculating the taxes due was described to Herskovits by informants telling what they knew of the traditions of a distant past. Men, women, boys and girls were counted, and for each individual a pebble was put in a sack marked by a design representing the appropriate category. An annual census was certainly taken, with whatever degree of accuracy. In addition there was a count of units of production of different kinds: grain stores for agriculture, palm trees for oil, forges for metal-working. Animals were taxed by numbers. According to the account given to Herskovits the owners made their own returns; that is, they were required to produce a cowrie for each animal. Hunters were enumerated on the occasion of an annual ritual for their protective deity, at which each was given a knife to offer to the god. On the basis of the numbers issued, leaders of different bands were required in turn to supply the palace with all the game they caught for a fixed period of time. After palm oil replaced slaves as the principal export a special tax was imposed on it, the yield of which was divided among the principal chiefs.

When Skertchly managed to get away from Abomey and spend a little time on the real purpose of his visit—collecting entomological specimens—he went north to a recently conquered area in the Kong hills. Here an 'old caboceer'—a resident representative of the royal authority—showed him the local tribute that he was about to send to the capital. 'It consisted of a few jars of palm oil, bags of cotton, cowries, Guinea corn and large calabashes of yams'.

Whereas both Asante and Fulani Zazzau obtained significant revenues from death duties, the portion of a subject's possessions which the ruler took on his death, the claim made by the Dahomean king seems to have been purely symbolic. According to Le Hérissé, a dead man's movable property was brought to the palace to be displayed and then at once returned to his heirs. Although a proverb says that the king inherits 'even the fly-switch of a leper', supposedly such a man's only possession, it seems unlikely that every individual's property went through this procedure.

Before the opening of the Annual Customs, at which every man in the kingdom was supposed to be present, a representative of every taxable group, territorial or occupational, was expected to appear before the palace and present the amount due. This ceremony was the reaffirmation of the relationship of king and people that is characteristic of so much royal ritual. Of course it was performed, like its counterparts elsewhere, after the harvest during the slack agricultural season, but the peculiarity of the Dahomean ritual was that it focused not on the fertility of the land but on success in war; its immediate occasion was supposedly the return of the army from its latest campaign. A great part of it consisted in the distribution of cowries and of imported goods, cloth, and liquor. Formal presentations were made to chiefs and to commoners who had distinguished themselves in fighting, and then, for hours at a time, and on several days, strings of cowries and lengths of cloth were thrown down from a raised platform to be scrambled for. When Skertchly witnessed this in 1871 nobles as well as commoners took part in the contest, and it may have had a ritual significance. Argyle notes that the objects distributed were those regarded as appropriate for sacrifice. It appears too that, despite the genuine ferocity of the struggle, there was an idea that everyone should receive a share.

The Dahomeans themselves believed that most of what was demanded of them was redistributed at the Customs and that the ceremonies which their contributions made possible were important enough to justify the demands. According to Polanyi, who presents a rather idyllic picture of this 'redistributive economy', the royal treasury, where taxes paid in kind were stored, contained materials for building and road-making and iron to be issued to blacksmiths, as well as the wherewithal for 'payment in kind to diverse craftsmen'. In terms of material return to those who carried on the business of government, we can see that, in Dahomey as elsewhere, those in high authority were given the resources that enabled them to support the followers who did the menial work or oversaw it.

What is of special interest here is that for some purposes payments, even at the lowest levels, were made in currency (cowries) and not in kind. Carriers or messengers travelling away from home were given cowries to buy food at the markets along their route, where only cowries were accepted in payment, a fact from which it follows that they circulated among the village women who brought their cooked food for sale as well as in more grandiose transactions.

Revenues in Asante

Whereas the Dahomean king's claim to inherit his subjects' property seems to have been no more than a ritual assertion of ownership of 'the land and everything in it', in Asante and Zaria it was enforced quite literally. Wilks estimates that in Asante it produced the greater part of the revenues; and he argues also that men who enriched themselves by trading were held to be actually serving the Asantehene because of the share of their wealth that would ultimately go to him. The amount due was calculated in gold dust, but sometimes equivalents were accepted or demanded. Villages were handed over, sometimes to the king himself, sometimes to a chief who made a payment which the dead man's property could not meet. It is hardly appropriate to call this, as Wilks does, 'dealing in real estate'; granted that the chief of a village had claims on objects found on uncultivated land and the right to allocate it, what was transferred was political authority with the prestige that it carried and the material advantages in tribute and labour. In special cases the king might take skilled servants, not necessarily slaves; for example, on the death of a chief of Bekwae he customarily took from his retinue one gold-weigher and one sword-carrier. The proportion taken does not seem to have been fixed; some records of past holders of chiefdoms mention a half or a third of their estate as due to the Asantehene, while in the case of the various state servants mentioned in the previous chapter the king, who had maintained and enriched them, took the whole. Divisional chiefs made corresponding claims on their subjects and servants. In turn king and chiefs made gifts at a dead subject's funeral, but these would be a small proportion of what they took from the estate. A successor to office made a payment, and in cases where the holder had been exempted from death duties as a special privilege the payment demanded was higher.

When gold dust was to be melted down to make ornaments, the king claimed one-fifth of the amount so used; his share may actually have been more, since the royal weights were heavier than those used by ordinary people. Gold nuggets were claimed by the divisional chief on whose land they were found, and from him by the king. They were reduced to dust by the royal goldsmiths in Kumase, after which the king took his share and returned the rest to be divided between the finder and his chief; according to some of Rattray's informants, chiefs and their elders took it all. Late in the nineteenth century the king Mensa Bonsu levied half the proceeds of all gold-mines.

A flat rate tax of one-tenth of an ounce of gold was due from every married man. In the late nineteenth century this was collected by emissaries from the capital, who received one-seventh of the proceeds in payment, the rest being divided equally between the king and the headman of the village where it was raised. Fines for letting the roads get blocked seem to have brought in considerable revenue; this was called 'sweeping money'. The king took a third of it, and the rest went to the road overseers and their head in Kumase. Tolls have been discussed in connection with the organization for collection.

Some kings raised special levies to finance military campaigns, but the payment that Wilks rather curiously calls a war tax was an indemnity imposed on defeated rebels and on peoples conquered for the first time. Another occasion for a special levy was the accession of a new king, and of some divisional chiefs, 'to replenish the treasury' as Rattray puts it (1929: 230), that is to let them embark on office with adequate resources, 'to feed them' as the Dahomeans would have put it.

From these revenues a bureaucracy that was apparently more numerous than that of any of the other kingdoms—unless this impression merely reflects the greater volume of information available—was rewarded essentially by commissions on what was collected. Records refer to arbitrary extortion only in the periods when control from Kumase was ineffective. Bowdich noted early in the century that royal messengers had been instructed to pay a fair price for the food needed on their journeys, though he did not ask whether this was paid to individuals or to local chiefs who requisitioned it. At times people complained of the obligation to supply men for the army, and the major count against Mensa Bonsu, the king who was deposed in 1883, was that he imposed excessive taxes and fines. But this complaint came from the wealthier section of the population, those who were frustrated in their desire to accumulate even greater wealth by the state trading monopoly and the levying of death duties.

In Fulani Zaria taxes were levied on grain, on hoes, and later on trade by means of tolls and market dues, including a tax on slaves sold. Kings expected to receive gifts from their officials on their own accession and on the latter's appointment, and this became formalized as a payment demanded (the king himself had to make such payments to the Sultan of Sokoto). They took a share of every official's property when he died, a claim that might be justified by the argument that it was the gift of office that had enabled him to acquire his property, and also from every vassal chief. From his own officials the king took one-sixth of their houses, cattle, and slaves, and from vassal chiefs a third of the slaves and cattle and half the childless concubines. When he dismissed an official he took half his property. He also claimed half of all booty taken in war.

In the discussion so far slaves have been referred to in passing as if they were just another commodity. Of course this is not so, and of course it was not only for the sake of the slave-trade that Dahomey fought its annual wars and that all the kingdoms demanded a quota of slaves as tribute from their vassals. Slaves played an important part in the internal economy. Wilks delicately refers to the employment of 'unfree labour' as carriers for trade goods as well as in production. Those who owned large numbers established them in villages where they produced food to support their masters living in the capital, and, later, export crops; the king of Dahomey's palm plantations were worked by his slaves. Kings of Zaria had slave settlements which were crown property and passed from one ruler to the next (it must be remembered that in Zaria three lineages claimed the succession in turn). Slaves too, then, formed part of the resources of the state, both in that the rulers everywhere disposed of those who were brought in as captives or as tribute, and, in Zaria and Asante, in that they were taken as death duties.

The revenues of Zaria had to meet the tribute demanded by Sokoto, the return for which was the payer's maintenance in office but no particular benefit for his subjects. They supported the royal household, rewarded officials, and maintained state property, including horses and weapons for the army. But they also served to enrich the lineage which was on the throne for the time being, and to reward the personal support, for example in backing the king's election from among the leading men of his lineage, of clients who had not been appointed to office. Perhaps it was not entirely hypocritical of the British to suppose that the proceeds of taxation might be expended in ways that would distribute their benefit more widely.

Which of the interpretations of the claims made by kings on their subjects mentioned at the beginning of this chapter is a sound evaluation must remain a matter of the reader's judgement. Those to whom the state is always and everywhere an organization for the extortion of surplus value will have no difficulty in deciding. Others face the difficulty of quantifying intangibles. Refusal to pay tribute could be punished by the burning and looting of villages and towns. Was it the 'common man' who instigated the refusal, or the vassal chief who preferred to keep the tribute for himself? Safe travel was an advantage for everyone, not only for wealthy traders; so were judicial institutions. African states did not reckon to provide their subjects with schools, hospitals, or clean water; from the time when their European overlords tried to persuade them to do so, there have been endless references to the high proportion of the budget devoted to salaries. For the period before the notion of social services reached Africa, however, the question to be asked is whether the common man had to pay too much for the minimum conditions of personal security; and nobody has yet produced a formula for a cost-benefit analysis of this kind.

CHAPTER VIII
THE BALANCE OF POWER

EARLIER chapters have discussed the process by which some individual claiming kingship has established a position of dominance over other leaders of groups, formerly his equals, who thus became his subjects, and that by which one ethnic group has extended domination over the territory of its neighbours. Of course these processes must have gone on side by side. There is a temptation to take the most recent account of any kingdom as if it described a constitution deliberately devised with checks and balances. Checks and balances there certainly were, but it may well be, as Peter Lloyd (1971) suggests, that they simply represent, as we know of them, the stage that had been reached, in the see-saw between king and chiefs, at the moment when colonial rule put an end to it—not, as with the earlier empires, by destroying the kingdoms, but by suppressing the power struggle and then imposing constitutional changes of a quite new type. It is true that such historical record as we have seems to describe a linear movement rather than an ebb and flow of central power; yet every time we read of the deposition of a king, or of the execution of conspirators against him, we are reminded that any particular contest could go one way or the other. And such rebellions as we read of are as likely, or more so, to have had their roots in the rejection of royal authority by chiefs defending their own privileges as in the resentment of oppressed peasants.

In most kingdoms, as anthropologists have been able to see or reconstruct them, kings have been expected to listen to the views of specified groups of people, forming councils which often have their distinctive names. In most kingdoms there have been specified persons with the right and responsibility of nominating the successor to a dead king, and even where succession is supposedly regulated by strict rules, the people in charge of the installation of the new ruler have *de facto* influence. In many kingdoms the ruler depends on the co-operation of priests whose ritual powers derive their validity from sources outside his control. A curious feature of many, which has already been discussed in connection with ritual, is the independent voice allowed, in particular contexts, to the king's closest female relatives, his mother and sister.

Although the Yoruba kings recognized a common ritual head in the Alafin of Oyo, he did not exercise political control over them, and no one of them controlled a very extensive domain; some were only heads of one town with its outliers, though the towns themselves, with populations of 10,000 or more, were large by the standards of pre-colonial Africa. Doubtless there is a connection between this fact and the narrow limits set to the authority of the kings. Peter Lloyd describes them as 'sacred'; this avoids the connotations that have been attached to the word 'divine' by readers of *The Golden Bough*. The firm basis of an Oba's authority was the sacredness conferred on him at his installation, which in itself guaranteed, in the eyes of the general populace, that he 'could do no wrong'. His sacredness could be diminished, however, if he was held to have lost the favour of the deities; and this question was answered by an oracle that he did not control.

The day-to-day conduct of public affairs was not in his hands, but in those of bodies of title-holders which were in some cases unusually representative. As Lloyd (1960) describes the organization of Ado Ekiti, there were five kingmakers, the Olori Marun, each of whose titles was hereditary within one of the major lineages. They formed the senior grade of an association of twenty chiefs, some of whom represented less important lineages while others were appointed by the Big Five in consultation with the Oba. This body itself was the highest of three grades of chiefs, the members of each of which held meetings at which they discussed public affairs, and then submitted their conclusions to the next highest grade. The Olori Marun themselves met daily in the courtyard of the palace, but usually without the Oba; their views were transmitted to him, and it was taken for granted that he would promulgate them, thereby giving them the support of his ritual authority.

Commonly, though apparently not in Ado, important ritual

powers were exercised by the *ogboni*, a cult association whose myths and rites were kept strictly secret, as were also its discussions of secular matters. The name *ogboni* is derived from words meaning 'elder'. Senior holders of secular titles had to join *ogboni*, and so did the members of trading associations where these existed.

The political activities of *ogboni*, and its relation with the kingmakers—here called Oyo Misi—in Oyo, have been described by Morton-Williams (1960). At the time of his inquiries a Muslim Alafin had recently disbanded his *ogboni*, but they were still flourishing in the Egbado kingdoms. The Oyo Misi, like the Olori Marun in Ado, met daily by themselves, not in the palace but in the house of their own leader, and then went together to give their advice to the Alafin. But every sixteenth day they joined in discussion with the rest of the *ogboni*, and in these gatherings they were cut off from the lineages of which each was the political representative and merged in a larger body whose deliberations were kept strictly secret. Differences of view within it could not be made public, and the Oyo Misi, like all the other members, were under the obligation to support its decisions. In the Egbado kingdoms the ritual head of the *ogboni* was also the priest of the oracle which was consulted every year to see whether the king still stood in favour with the gods and so should continue to rule; and in the smaller of them the *ogboni* had themselves taken over the functions of the Oyo Misi.

Not every king was content to be a mere mouthpiece. How far a king could assert himself depended largely on the strength of his palace following, particularly of slaves. The 'citizen army' which fought in foreign wars was recruited by the different chiefs from among their own followers. Intrigue, says Lloyd (1960), was a king's chief weapon. He was able to reward his loyal supporters by the grant of titles, and this could not be formally opposed by bodies of chiefs as it could in Benin. So his subjects sometimes found they had more to gain by revealing plots against him than by joining in them.

Ado chiefs might boycott the palace, if they could all agree—but there was no *ogboni* association there to compel agreement. Such action implied a boycott of the rituals which were performed in the palace. Hence it was a double-edged weapon, for if the chiefs prevented the performance of rituals on which the general welfare was believed to depend, they could themselves be held responsible for anything that was going wrong.

A Yoruba Oba, then, was not a priest-king whose main significance lay in his ritual activities. He had ritual powers not shared by any of his subjects; he could curse those who disobeyed him and forbid them entry to the palace, thus (in some cases) debarring them from political discussions. He was the symbol of established order, so that an Oba could say without contradiction—as one did on the death of George VI— 'When we try to dispense with the position of king we immediately find the town with the people concerned thrown into confusion; we find lawlessness and general disorder'.

Another country where a body of ritual experts was the main counterbalancing force to the king's power was Rwanda, where the college of *abiru* was responsible for his installation and for the rites he was expected to perform for the general welfare. Exceptionally, the Rwanda ritual was secret; but the nation had to be told that it had been successfully carried out, so that here too neither the king nor any of the *abiru* could afford to be intransigent in blocking them. It also rested with the *abiru* to name the lineage from which the king should choose his royal consort, ostensibly in accordance with an ancestrally ordained rotation.

Yet another category of ritual experts on whose goodwill a ruler might depend were the earth-priests or 'owners of the land', who in many parts of West Africa tended shrines that were reputedly older than those of the reigning dynasty. Their position has been described most fully in the context of the Bariba kingdoms in the north of Dahomey, kingdoms founded by the emigration from Borgu of bands of mounted huntsmen led by princes who, like the Zande or Luba chiefs, constantly sought to set up their own principalities independently of their fathers. The populations over which they established their rule recognized ritual heads, perhaps with minimal political power but with a monopoly of access to the local deities. As Lombard (1965: 183) puts it, the conquerors never sought to take over those ritual functions. One might say they hardly could, so universal is the belief that local divinities 'belong to' those who have lived longest under their protection—were it not for the annexation of the *abiru* by a Rwanda king. But the 'compact' recorded in Bariba traditions, whether it was historical or mythical, left to the 'owners of the soil' their religious authority and also gave them the right, as priests of the earth in which Bariba kings would be buried, to conduct their funerals and also their accession rites. In practice the kings looked to the earth-priests as their intermediaries with the spirits for whatever purpose; and made gifts to them which included insignia of office, sandals, Arab-style clothes, and sometimes even a horse.

In Rwanda we are not told much about the discussion of secular matters. The accounts of most kingdoms describe councils which gathered at the royal capital, but there are differences in their 'constitutional' status—in the extent to which they could claim a right to be heard and in the degree to which, like the Yoruba secular councils, they could be considered to represent the views of different sections of the population.

In Buganda the chiefs who were expected to maintain houses at the royal capital brought news to the king of events and conditions in the areas they governed, but the most recent studies indicate that they did not constitute a formal council until they were 'recognized' as a law-making body by the British authorities. There was not here any obligation on the king to consult them. Sir Apolo Kaggwa, who around 1900 compiled a history of the kings of Buganda, records an occasion, probably in the seventeenth century, when King Mutebi planned to dismiss two important chiefs who had been appointed by his predecessor; he summoned a council to ask their advice, and it was that this would be a difficult thing to do (cited Southwold n.d.: 9–10). Since the kingdoms were not thought of as the property of a royal lineage, there was equally no obligation to consult close agnates, as there was in some Southern Bantu chiefdoms. In the Interlacustrine Bantu kingdoms, the king's sons were required to live at a distance from the court, and only summoned to the capital when the time came to nominate a successor; and some Ganda kings had their brothers put to death as soon as they had sons to make the succession secure.

Nevertheless, these kings did not bear the sole weight of decision, or exercise untramelled despotism, whichever interpretation one prefers. Each of them had a 'favourite counsellor', a commoner who has often been described in English as a 'prime minister'. A new king retained his predecessor's adviser and was expected to be guided by him. He would eventually be superseded by someone of this king's own choice. But this need not imply that such a man was a mere sycophant.

The Ganda Katikkiro, however, was the most important man in the kingdom after the king himself, and had territorial authority over a wide area. He was responsible, as was the Nkole *nganzi* (literally 'favourite') for the installation of his master's successor. Maquet remarks that one of the most important functions of the 'favourite counsellor' was to take the blame for any cause of dissatisfaction, leaving the king himself out of reach of criticism; and it is certainly interesting that many people who were wedded to the idea of monarchy—including some in quite recent centuries in Europe—have liked to believe that whatever goes wrong is the fault not of the king but of his 'evil counsellors'.

The kings of Rwanda are said to have summoned their leading chiefs for consultation, though Maquet (1961: 128) holds that this was to get their views on how to implement decisions already taken rather than on what should be done. In such a council the men who had to be listened to were the *abiru*, the guardians of ritual secrets who have been mentioned in Chapter II. Although, as was pointed out there, it was an effective political move to take over the *abiru* as guarantors of royal legitimacy, the price paid for it was to give them an influence that was not easy to resist. The first *abiru* had been hereditary rulers who were confirmed as subject authorities, and though later ones were the creation of Rwanda kings, they could effectively claim hereditary status since the secret knowledge that each of them possessed was preserved by passing it on within his lineage; it was not politically possible to transfer the office of a *mwiru* to a more amenable individual. Their most powerful weapon was their knowledge of the correct ritual for the installation of a king; they might use this retrospectively to argue that a reigning king's position was not valid. Also it was for them to say from what lineage the queen must be taken. Logically, they might thwart the king's designs by refusing to perform the rites for which they were responsible, but the value of this strategy was limited by the fact that they could themselves be blamed if they delayed some ritual that was held to be necessary for the general welfare.

The Ngambela of the Lozi was his king's chief *induna*, to use a Zulu word that became current further north as a result both of Ngoni and of South African expansion. In a kingdom where princes were not debarred from political power it was important that he could not be a member of the royal lineage. Gluckman (1951: 46–7) interprets his role as that of the people's representative to the king; his homestead was a sanctuary for anyone who had incurred the royal anger. But the king himself was also, in a manner that Gluckman does not specify, the protector of the people against the Ngambela. He was not the king's sole adviser, for there was an elaborate council organization; but he presided over the full council and reported its deliberations to the king, who returned his answer to them through him.

Unlike many ethnographers, Gluckman gives an indication of the kind of matter that the council might discuss. The most momentous of all were questions of war and peace, but if large public works were planned, such as digging a canal or building one of the mounds on which Lozi made their villages, the council would have to consider whether there was enough food available for the workers. Then there was appointment to titled offices, which one might guess would be the most hotly disputed of all. But Gluckman remarks that the divisions of the council which deliberated separately were not based on opposed economic interests; so that whether their conclusions did or did not coincide would be a matter of individual views. This would seem to have been true of most of the kingdoms with multiple councils, though M. G. Smith (1960) writes of Zazzau as if its two councils did represent different interests.

The full council of the Lozi had three divisions known as 'mats' from the placing of the mats on which the members sat.

On the right of the royal dais were the senior indunas, men who had judicial and executive authority over divisions of the Lozi people (these were not territorial divisions, a peculiar feature of Lozi polity); on the left were the 'stewards', officials responsible for the collection of tribute, for which purpose the general population was divided in a different way; and still further to the left were the royal princes. The councillors of each 'mat' sat in strict order of the seniority of their titles, and they spoke in order from junior to senior, so that no one was ever in the position of contradicting a senior. Out of this council were formed three bodies in each of which there were members of every 'mat'. Two of these, the Saa and Katengo, represented respectively the senior and junior members of the three 'mats', and so might be expected to come to different conclusions on some matters; the head of Katengo, however, was a member of Saa. The third included the highest chiefs of all, the Ngambela and the Natamoyo, the latter the only prince to sit on the mat-of-the-right; his title means 'giver of life', but Gluckman does not describe his functions. With them were 'an undetermined number' (Gluckman 1951: 50) of senior chiefs. Messages would pass between these councils, and their aim was to reach an agreed view to put before the king.

In the West African cases which are on record, separate consultative bodies were not expected to agree, and M. G. Smith envisages in Zazzau a process in which either the two such bodies were in agreement to oppose the king, or he got his way with the support of one of the two (of course there is no reason why all three should not sometimes have agreed). The total number of people whom the king of Zazzau was expected to consult was small: first the four senior officials of his own household and then the holders of the four senior public offices. The only kind of business that Smith mentions is the conferment of titles and appointment to offices, and it is clear that this was a matter of much more interest than administrative decisions, while one might almost say that there were no issues of general policy. Public offices might be filled either by the promotion of existing public officials or by transfer from the royal household. It was by infiltrating the public offices that the palace officials could increase their influence, but it is not at all clear what would be the issues that would interest them as a body. One might suspect that individuals of both sections backed men from whom they expected personal favours. Where the two councils disagreed, Smith tells us, the king could do as he chose; but it would be instructive to follow the fortunes of a man appointed to any post against the wishes of those senior in authority to him.

Bradbury (1973) had the advantage of being able to draw on the memories of living men for his record of the power struggles that went on in Benin in the context of the elaborate structure of separate yet interlocking councils described in Chapter IV. No doubt the complexity of the system as it was described to him reflected the outcome of such struggles in a past too distant to be traced. It is clear from his account that they were pure power contests, focused on the control of titles and the resources that went with them and not on any general issues such as would deserve the name of policy. The opposition between the claims of king and subjects that is found in some form in all kingdoms had its own mythical charter in Benin: the story that the ruling dynasty was founded by a prince brought from Oyo, who had to leave his kingdom after begetting a son because the Edo would not endure the rule of a foreigner. Hence the opposition between town and palace chiefs was represented as the defence of the Edo against the foreign ruler and his retainers, or, in terms of principles, the defence of 'the commonalty against the threat of palace autocracy' (Bradbury 1973: 79). Bradbury does see the three orders of chiefs as corporate bodies each trying to extend its own influence; and in contexts in which each order was called on to express a collective opinion they would have to agree on a common line. But he also takes account of internal rivalries and of the common interests that might link members of the different orders, and concludes that in actual conflicts the alignment of factions was very fluid. Nevertheless, crises in the kingdom were represented in tradition as confrontations between the king and *Iyase*, the senior town chief, who alone had the right to oppose the king in public. The town chiefs, as well as the hereditary *Uzama*, the official 'guardians of custom', had ritual responsibilities on the performance of which the sacred aspect of the Oba's power depended. Although the ultimate validation of his sacredness was his royal descent, the mystical power to maintain the welfare of the nation that only he possessed could not be sustained without periodic renewal through the many ceremonies which punctuated the year.

In earlier days, it is said, the *Uzama* chiefs were the Oba's principal opponents, and the eventual assertion of royal supremacy over them was commemorated in a ritual that included a mock battle ending with their submission. Their formal assent was required for all royal decisions, and their part in the installation of a new king was indispensable. At one time they had actually chosen the king, but by the nineteenth century the rule of primogeniture had come to be recognized, and although this did not prevent wars for the succession, it much reduced the influence of the *Uzama* over the choice. One of them, the *Ezomo*, was a war commander, and as such the equal in power of the *Iyase*. But each of these had a deputy from another order. The *Uzama* as a body did not take much part in public discussion.

There was yet another form of power-sharing, in connection with foreign trade. Police authority over the beaches where trading canoes put in, and over the port of Ughoton where European ships called, was in the hands of two senior palace chiefs from the *Ibiwe* association. But the trade itself was in the hands of other associations, each controlling one of the routes, and these contained members of all the chiefly orders, who did not depend for their membership on appointment but simply on ability to pay the necessary fees. This trade was a more important source of wealth than the tribute or gifts of villagers; from it came the resources that enabled men to buy slaves. It was men who had been successful in these associations who obtained rapid promotion into the ranks of the town chiefs.

It is from Asante, where we have rich documentary records going back before the nineteenth century, that we know most about the actual issues that divided the makers of decisions. Those of which we learn most are matters of foreign relations, as we should expect since most of the documents are the work of Europeans dealing with Asante kings. From early times English writers have discussed Asante politics in terms current at home. This illustrates a conception of the kingdom that was appropriate at the period when Europeans dealt with African states by negotiation and not dictation. But when Asante institutions are described in a twentieth-century vocabulary, as they are by Wilks, one is baffled in the same way as one would be if it were applied to the Tudor or Stuart monarchies. Nevertheless it is possible to see past Bowdich's references to 'three estates', the 'aristocracy', and the 'Privy Council', and Wilks's to government of opposing parties, to a fairly clear idea of what qualified the holders of particular positions to have a voice in decisions.

The 'assembling of the nation', as the word that Wilks renders by 'parliament' is literally translated, did not consist, as did the councils previously described, of people living permanently in the capital. It included, in addition to the senior Kumase chiefs, the heads of all the states of which metropolitan Asante was composed. These were summoned once a year on the occasion of the great yam festival (*Odwira*), as were the rulers of vassal kingdoms, who, however, sometimes sent representatives. The council could also be called together at other times; one such occasion arose when Dwaben rebelled. As Wilks sees it, a major matter for deliberation was the apportionment of responsibility for providing men and gold for war campaigns; and this could well lead to argument about mounting a campaign at all. Bonnat, the French trader who was held as a hostage in Kumase from 1869 to 1874, wrote that the Asantehene 'must attend to all the petty affairs of his kingdom, and furthermore to religion, to commerce, to agriculture, to weights and measures, to prices and tariffs of all kinds' (cited Wilks 1975: 392).

Even the capitals of the 'five great towns' were two days' journey from Kumase; not only was it a time-consuming process to summon the council and gather it together, but all those who had a right to be there did not always care to make the journey. This in itself would be likely to lead to the development of the smaller body that Bowdich called the 'Privy Council', and Wilks calls the Inner Council which, he says, later became the Council of Kumase. Bowdich said in 1821 that there were four councillors 'whom the king always consults on the creation or repeal of a law; whose interference in foreign politics or in questions of war or tribute amount to a veto on the king's decisions . . . and whose power as an estate of the government always keeps alive the jealousy of the General Assembly' (Bowdich 1821: 22, cited Wilks 1975: 395). These officials were the heads of wards in Kumase; one of them was the Gyaasewahene or treasurer, whose responsibilities were described in Chapter VI. All these were appointive, not hereditary, officials. According to Bowdich the king could not decide matters of war and peace without their agreement (in practice he would need the agreement of at least two of them). But in other questions they would 'watch rather than share' in decisions. In addition there were two senior *akyeame* (see Chapter VI), and other chiefs with special knowledge of the matters under discussion would be invited to attend.

In 1870, when the Asantehene had to decide whether to hand over his three European hostages to the British or hold them for the ransom he had originally demanded, the council met every day except on holy days. By this time it was larger, and, as the missionary hostage Kühne understood it, the members were heads of the various bureaucratic organizations, not (or not primarily) holders of territorial authority. It now included (naturally) military leaders and the heads of the royal physicians (who were also practitioners of magic), the treasury and the sword-bearers, as well as a representative of the royal lineage and four *akyeame*. The queen mother, whose special position must be discussed further, also had a voice. There was no idea, however, that either the total number or the status of members was permanently fixed.

The West African kingdoms maintained their independence in relation to European states for much longer than most of the others, and the question of confrontation or negotiation and accommodation, of war and peace, was for them a matter of serious debate. This was doubtless true of Benin and Dahomey, but it is from Asante that we have the fullest records. If these do not necessarily support Wilks's interpretation of conflicting views as the expression of permanently opposed economic interests, they do show when conflicts arose and how decisions were reached. The many Europeans who recorded their observations could see that the Asantehene's councils were dominated at different times by the advocates of different policies, and that he was not in a position to reject views that had strong support despite the fact that by tradition he, like other monarchs, had the last word. There was of course room for diplomacy. 'I must do what the old men say', Osei Bonsu told Dupuis in 1820; but the same Dupuis records that he was determined to have his way.

There was certainly no absolute commitment to the principle of democratic discussion. More than once a king's opponents plotted to depose him, were discovered and large numbers put to death; though it is not always certain that their motive was their attitude towards the question of war or peace. As has happened in other parts of the world, the king's enemies would attach themselves to his presumptive successor, and in the choice of a new Asantehene, a matter that was not determined by strict rules in Asante any more than in the other kingdoms, a candidate's attitude on this question was of some importance. We should need more evidence, though, to be sure that this was the crucial division between the supporters of rival princes.

The special status of the mothers and sisters of kings has been considered in connection with royal ritual, and their secular importance was inevitably mentioned in that context, but it deserves a little more discussion here.

In Asante, where, under a system of matrilineal succession, it was through his mother and not his father that a king derived his claim to the Golden Stool, one would expect the queen-mother to have an important position. But the woman who held the title generally so translated—that of Asantehemaa—obtained it as one who was qualified to be, not one who actually was, the mother of a king. The first Asantehemaa was the daughter of Osei Tutu's eldest sister, the second the daughter of his second sister; all the later ones traced their descent through their mothers to her. The actual successor to the office was chosen from a number of princesses, as the king was from a number of princes. She might be the king's sister. Once appointed she would use her influence to secure the succession for one of her own sons. The queen-mother was a respected member of the council, and presided over it when the king was away with his army. Several queen-mothers are on record as speaking on the side of peace in the debates of the nineteenth century. But they also sometimes joined in plots against their royal 'sons', and some lost their lives as a result.

The 'mothers' of Yoruba and Dahomey officials are not described as exercising any particular political influence. But the Bariba kingdoms offer us a remarkable instance of a royal woman whose ritual functions had political implications. This lady was called the 'senior princess'. She was not in fact the eldest of the king's sisters or daughters, but had the title conferred on her by the king with the agreement of his close kin. Usually she was chosen from a branch of the royal line other than that of the reigning king. Her title literally meant 'the elder of the razors', and it referred to the fact that at the annual national ceremony it fell to her to shave the heads of the young boys (about seven years old) of the royal lineage and to give to each the name of one of his ancestors. The name supposedly indicated that the fortunes of its bearer would correspond to those of his predecessor and so foretold his chances of success in competition for the kingship; conferred as it was on a ritual occasion, it was regarded as an expression of the ancestors' choice, not simply that of the princess. To have a propitious name did not guarantee the succession, since in the Bariba kingdoms this was contested by force of arms, but it was one of the considerations that secured support for a candidate, and to that extent the senior princess did have an influence in politics.

Among the Bantu kingdoms the most interesting from this point of view is that of the Lozi. They had two capitals of identical construction twenty-five miles apart, which represented a division of the kingdom into north and south. The southern one was ruled by a sister of the king whom Gluckman calls the 'princess-chief', and was a sanctuary from the king's anger. The princess-chief had her own chiefs and councillors and her own army, and she was consulted on all matters of importance. But the princess-chief of Gluckman's day told him that though she might argue against the king she would not hold out against him; nor would she try to get her way by refusing to perform her ritual duties.

It is in this context more than in any other that one feels the absence of written records contemporary with events. The contrast between the lively picture of Asante politics and the stylised accounts of constitutional arrangements remembered when the kings had lost their independence is striking. Outside Asante we know of principles, we can talk of possibilities, some writers have been able to interpret such meagre evidence as records of the succession to chiefly titles. But we know enough to see that no monarch was absolute and that positions of countervailing power were generally recognized, possibly because no king was able wholly to destroy them. It is perhaps most instructive to see the importance of religious belief not only as an ideology but as a check on political power; if access to spiritual beings is a resource, it is of a very different kind from those that are commonly considered in the discussion of power struggles.

CHAPTER IX
SUCCESSION CONTESTS

EVEN where there are ostensibly precise rules of succession to kingship, people will find means to contest it as long as the office is desirable. It would be an exaggeration to say that the strict rules which hold in Britain were not established until the throne ceased to be a source of political power, but it is only since that time that monarchs have stepped into their predecessors' shoes without any argument about claims. In African kingdoms it was exceptional for succession rules to designate a single individual; in the majority of cases a choice was made between a number of eligible candidates, and in some of them the contest was expected to be one of armed force. Wherever there was to be a contest, princes would be gathering support some time ahead, perhaps all through their adult lives. A further complication in some African kingdoms was that the succession went in turn to different branches of the royal lineage, or even to different independent lineages. Where this was the rule, a candidate would have to seek support within his own descent group, by pacific means and not by fighting, but there was still sometimes argument between the branches as to whose turn was next.

Succession Qualifications

Although a prince could not become a king without going through a rite of passage of the kind described in Chapter III, the belief that only a member of the royal lineage could be qualified could have its ritual aspect. Thus the Yoruba held that a pretender who went through the accession ceremonies would die—that is that only a legitimate successor would be ritually strong enough to receive the powers that they conferred. But very many people might have the basic ritual qualification, whatever it was, that went with royal descent, particularly since kings and princes, with their many wives, had many sons. The number of possible claimants could not be allowed to increase indefinitely. It was usually limited by the rule that only a man whose own father had reigned could be a claimant—and this rule might stimulate competition among the sons of kings, each aware that, if he failed, his descendants would be disqualified for ever.

In many African states there were kingmakers, who selected one of the eligible royals and presented him to a gathering of the people. Sometimes they purported to be acting on the wishes of the dead king, as did the leading *abiru* in Rwanda. In Buganda the successor was chosen by the senior chiefs, purely secular officials with no hereditary status. Benin provided for the nomination in advance of the chosen heir, who should then have been included among the *Uzama* (see Chapter VIII), with the title of *Edaiken*; but in fact most kings of Benin were afraid to appoint a son to a position from which he might challenge their authority, and no Edaiken was appointed during the nineteenth century. Tradition said that strict primogeniture had been established early in the eighteenth century with the deliberate aim of avoiding contests; but in fact there are a number of recorded instances of such contests. In Dahomey too the kings were said, at any rate by some authorities, to nominate their successors, and the rule of succession from father to own son is said to have been introduced at the time when in Allada to the south, as in Borgu to the north, a number of lineages claimed to provide the king in turn. The heir had to be the son of a commoner woman, and must have no physical defect (left-handedness was regarded as one such). According to Argyle (1966: 58), oracles were consulted on his future prospects; M. A. Glélé (1974: 94), a member of the royal line, writes that the consultation was made at the time of the prince's birth, and the oracle then named the ancestor who would have an especial responsibility for him, and from whose life-story his destiny could be predicted. In such a case it would be for the king to take the prediction into account when he made his choice. Argyle tells us that it needed the approval of the two leading officials, the Migan and the Meu, though the evidence that he gives is the record of an occasion when these two set aside the chosen heir after his father's death, not quite the same thing.

The heir apparent shared power with his father. Of course there was rivalry for the office. M. A. Glélé refers to 'intrigues going as far as poisoning', and quotes a proverb which said 'The throne is always contested and seized in a struggle' (1974: 87).

Circulating Succession

In a number of West African kingdoms it was the rule that the kingship should circulate among several branches of the royal house, and in one, the Fulani kingdom of Zaria, four independent lineages claimed this right in virtue of the contribution of their founders to the conquest of the country. Zaria was a special case in that, as a vassal state of Sokoto, it had to accept the intervention of its overlord in matters which elsewhere were settled by internal power struggles. But we know so much more about the actual course of these struggles in Zaria, from the research of M. G. Smith (1965), than we do in relation to other kingdoms, that this system, anomalous as it is, deserves to be described first.

In Zaria, although the rule that a king should not be succeeded by a member of his own line was generally followed, there was not even a theoretical order of rotation, and two of the four eligible lines held the kingship for most of the nineteenth century. According to Smith, conventional rules of succession had come to be accepted after about fifty years of Fulani rule, but his own account shows that these were by no means always followed. Three officials were recognized as kingmakers: the senior non-royal territorial chief, the senior Muslim priest and the chief justice. They seem sometimes to have made their own nomination of one candidate and sometimes to have left it to Sokoto to choose from three candidates, the men they judged to have most support in each of the eligible lineages. The number of competitors was limited not only by the rule that only a man whose father had been king could succeed to the throne, but that to be eligible he must also have held a senior territorial chiefship; this rule led the kings to appoint as many of their sons as possible to such offices so that they should have a chance of the succession.

Records and memories tell little of the power struggles

within lineages which led to their choice of one man as candidate, though Smith mentioned that the chance of success in competition with rival lineages was a consideration. But we know a good deal about the means by which a king, once on the throne, made hay while the sun shone. In Zaria the conception of the kingship as a source of profit outweighed such considerations of duty to their subjects as we find among longer-established dynasties. On the death of a king who had reigned for only a few weeks, it was argued that his lineage had not had their share of power, and Sokoto supported the claim of a successor from the same line. As far as they were able, kings, on their accession, dismissed incumbents from the leading offices and substituted their own close kin.

But after a time their power to do this was restricted by the interference of Sokoto in appointments to superior chiefships as well as in the succession itself—a 'divide and rule' policy in the only meaningful sense of that phrase. From about 1880 Sokoto sought to weaken the king's power by keeping senior offices in the possession of other lineages than his. But since it did not specify the individuals to be appointed, a counter-measure was available in deliberately appointing weak characters. This, however, had the disadvantage that the duties of the office were not done efficiently, and the king could not rely on the exercise of the chief's authority, even though he might be sure he would not be actively sabotaged. Sambo, the king at this period, tried to secure his position by making a Habe client governor of Zaria as well as Galadima (the senior non-royal chiefship). He thought he could count on the loyalty of a man who owed everything to him, but he had merely created an over-mighty subject who eventually rebelled against him.

For various reasons, not all connected with rivalry for the succession, Sambo was deposed by Sokoto and succeeded by Yero, whose father Abdullahi sixty years earlier had been deposed, reinstated, and then deposed again. The property of a deposed ruler was divided between the Sultan and his successor. Thus Yero, though he had lost an earlier individual inheritance, had had his share of Sambo's wealth. However, he determined to recover what he could of his father's possessions by plundering the lineage to whom they had gone, and to this end he built up a force of slaves armed with guns which he bought from the Royal Niger Company. They did not confine their attentions strictly to Yero's rivals. However, as Smith indicates (1965: 192), their activities simply carried to a logical extreme the principle that the estates of a rival lineage were liable to confiscation as its members were dismissed from office. Yero expected his successor, whoever he might be, to retaliate in kind, and he evaded this crude form of death duty by giving a large slave village to his son. It is hard to guess what this practice might have led to if Zaria had remained independent, but Yero's successor, Kwassau, appealed to the British to defend him against his neighbours, and so found himself under a more demanding overlord.

The British, while purporting to recognize traditional rules of succession, did not follow them closely, and they appointed three successive kings from the same lineage, all of them men whose fathers had not ruled. But they severely cut down the number of territorial chiefs, and as they regarded administrative experience as an important qualification for the kingship, this imposed a new limit on the number of candidates. Now there developed the same demand for rotation between the segments of a single lineage as there had been before for rotation between lineages. So, within a narrower range, the same process of eliminating rivals and rewarding supporters went on. The approved reasons for dismissing a chief from office had changed. For the British, only shortcomings in bureaucratic or financial probity could justify it. But it was not hard to find grounds for charges of this kind. At the same time, a great many new bureaucratic offices were created as technical services (health, education, agriculture, veterinary) were developed; the senior posts were filled by the king from his kin and clients, the lower ones by the heads of departments on the same principle.

The Muslim kingdoms alone in Africa possessed a specialized judiciary in the mallams with their expert knowledge of Koranic law. They were in theory politically neutral, and they were largely so in fact. But they were never conceived as a countervailing force to royal power. This was what the British meant by the independence of the judiciary; and in addition they developed a system of courts which called for the appointment of many more judges. The post of chief justice soon came to circulate among a number of lineages.

It was now possible for supporters of the king to be dismissed by a judge on grounds that would be upheld by the British authorities. The king could not dismiss the chief justice, and only the chief justice could appoint and dismiss his subordinates. So the king had to find means of protecting his kinsmen and followers. The readiest was to promote the chief justice to a post outside the judicial system. Another stratagem was to appoint kin of the chief justice to departmental offices, thus making them in effect hostages for his compliance with the king's wishes.

In Allada succession went in turn to five different lineages, and Glélé, in arguing the merits of direct succession in Dahomey, remarks that the French were able to establish their control there by intervening in a dispute between rival claimants. Lombard shows how in Borgu a similar rule contributed to the process of endless division that was still going on at the time when France and Britain partitioned the country. He has reconstructed from oral tradition a picture of endless power struggles between princes who devoted their entire adult life to the contest. They were seeking the royal status which only a king could pass on to his heirs; not, like Zande or Luba princes, an autonomy that they could achieve by conquering new territory.

The aristocracy of the Borgu kingdoms had entered their present home as horsemen living by hunting and pillage, and the sons of a king maintained this way of life up to the moment when one was chosen to succeed his father. The many who were unsuccessful could be appointed to administer divisions of the kingdom, and could pass these lower-ranking offices to their sons; and some gave up the struggle early and sought offices of this kind. Those who favoured their chances, however, gathered followers from their matrilateral kin, who could not be their rivals, and from anyone else who was attracted by the distribution of booty. When the choice came to be made, prestige in fighting and the actual command of power played a significant part.

But a prince's success did not depend entirely on his own efforts. Likely winners were marked in childhood, at the annual Gani festival when all nobles, princes and office-holders assembled to do homage and bring gifts to the king, and to 'salute the drums' in which dwelt the spirits of the royal ancestors. Each brought with him his young children to have conferred upon them by the senior princess (Gnon Kogi) an ancestral name which would predict for each a destiny similar to that of its previous holder. The prophecy of success might well be self-fulfilling; and in addition an illustrious name was believed to carry with it that ritual efficacy which is so widely believed to be essential for secular achievement.

If this represented a first selection, one which limited the contest to two or three candidates was made through the conferment of a high-ranking title by the king. These titles, passed down in the royal lineage, carried no authority, but the highest, those which were said to 'open the door' to the throne, entitled the holders to ride caparisoned horses and use the copper stirrups of the ancestors who first held them. Rivals would fight or poison one another for nomination to these titles, for which they were put forward by the elders of the descent line which 'owned' them. The title designated the holder as the official choice of his branch of the royal line when its turn came for the kingship. But, like the Gani name, it was also held to confer an additional element of the ritual power to command success. Although the titles were supposedly ranked in order, a holder might try to enhance his status by going ahead of his turn to salute the ancestral drums; this too is remembered to have led to fighting.

Nor was the rule of rotation between the five branches of the royal line always strictly kept. The branch whose turn it was could be ousted by force, and the 'usurpers' would then maintain that they had followed what was really the correct order. This was the strategy of a candidate who had the support of his branch but was afraid he might not live till his turn came round; it was risky, because it made enemies, and he might, as Lombard (1965: 322) delicately puts it, lose by premature death what would have come to him if he had waited for it.

The system of rotation among the Gonja of northern Ghana,

as it is described by Jack Goody (1966), seems to have worked as smoothly in designating the successor as any system of primogeniture. Lineages succeeded in turn to territorial chiefships as well. Five territorial chiefs, each belonging to a different lineage, were entitled to succeed in turn to the kingship. Any office which fell vacant was filled by the senior man—not the oldest, but the holder of the senior title—of the lineage whose turn it was. A ritual assertion of the claim to succeed was made at a new king's installation, when, as he mounted his horse to return to the capital, the territorial chief whose lineage was next in line seized his bridle and led his horse on. At the lower level a chief was selected by the existing chiefs of his division; thus all the eligible lineages had their say, and the divisional chief could not favour his own kin as did the Fulani in Zazzau. Goody does mention the possibility of a disputed succession, though only in the case of divisional chiefs, for whom the system was still in operation when he was there in 1964. He sees it as having many advantages. In Gonja the territorial chiefs must stay in their own divisions up to the time when one becomes king and moves with his family and followers to the capital. But, because they all hope to succeed to the kingship, they are not tempted to assert their independence as, for example, the Zande princes were. They 'have a stake in seeing that the kingship to which they might eventually succeed is not damaged by attack from without or by succession from within' (Goody 1966: 162). The counter to any attempt by a ruling lineage to perpetuate its power would be not secession but rebellion by a combination of the rest. So it may be that those who regard direct succession as preferable are simply committing the error of ethnocentrism, of assuming that what is done in their own society must be best. Certainly there is no reason why a conflict between claimants in any system should not lead to foreign intervention.

The Nomination of the Heir

In Asante the rule of succession was matrilineal, that is a king derived the right to reign through his mother and not his father. It has been mentioned that the Asante recognized, alongside the Asantehene, a 'queen-mother', the Asantehemaa—not a mother of the ruling king but a sister whose son would be the next king. The rule that an Asantehene must be the son of an Asantehemaa was never broken. In this system the sons of kings were not themselves of royal lineage. But by marrying his sons to royal women—or rather by requiring royal women to marry his sons—a king could make his grandsons eligible for the Golden Stool, and in fact the kings of Asante did follow their grandfathers in a direct line. But since a son could not succeed his father two lines alternated. The second Asantehene, Opoku Ware, was the son of the first Asantehemaa, who was a sister's daughter of the first Asantehene Osei Tutu. Down to the eighth king the Golden Stool was held in turn by descendants of these two. Each king nominated as his successor a member of the other line—though this by no means always guaranteed the succession. It came to be taken for granted that senior women of the royal lineage should marry into one or other line. But early in the nineteenth century a lady who never expected to become Asantehemaa married a man of neither. Her son Kwaku Dua I succeeded in 1834, apparently without opposition. He nominated two heirs apparent, one from each of the claimant houses. But he did not let his sisters' daughters marry into these houses, so they were effectively barred from the succession; and he married six of his own sons to royal women.

To name an heir apparent was in itself hardly more than a gesture, since a dead king's wishes were not regarded as sacrosanct, and more than once a king died while his nominee was still a child. The formal procedure for the choice of an heir was for the Asantehemaa, after consulting with various persons in high authority, including the head of the treasury and the head of the police, to offer three names, in order of preference, to the council of Kumase chiefs—who, however, could reject them all. One would suppose that the choice would depend on their estimate of the candidates' support, and some of the records show clearly that this meant not popularity, let alone voting support, but military support. Perhaps this was how the succession was decided on the occasions when no contest is recorded. But eight out of fifteen kings of Asante up to the present day secured the Golden Stool by fighting.

Regents and Caretakers

One way of contending a succession, even one that has been ostensibly decided, is to claim that the king is in fact a caretaker appointed in the minority of a rival. Two of the more controversial of the Asante kings, Kofi Kakari (1867–75) and his younger brother Mensa Bonsu (1874–83), who were both removed from office, were described by Captain Barrow, a British envoy to Kumase, as having held their posts only 'at pleasure' of the grandson of Kwaku Dua I, whom he had nominated as heir apparent but who was only seven years old when he died. Barrow's report was made at the time when the charges that led to his destoolment were being brought against Mensa Bonsu, and one might guess that there was an element of hindsight in this assessment of the two brothers' status.

A better documented illustration of this kind of argument comes from some Tswana chiefdoms which have not been discussed in this book because their extent and organization did not seem to qualify them for the designation of kingdoms. These are the Rolong chiefdoms in one of the Bantu 'homelands' of South Africa, where J. L. Comaroff worked in 1969–70. The rules of succession of the Tswana, the group to which the Rolong belong, were such as to make a minority almost inevitable, since a chief's heir had to be the son of a woman whom he had married after his own accession. Their annals are full of wicked uncles who would not step down when a nephew came of age. Perhaps at any given time as many holders of office were regents as substantive chiefs. While in theory a substantive chief cannot be deposed, it is recognized that a regent may be, and that it is for the people to decide when he must give way to the recognized heir. The effect of this principle is that the status accorded to a chief depends upon genealogical argument. If it is agreed that he had in fact the right qualifications when he succeeded, well and good; if not, then he must only be a regent usurping the place of a 'rightful heir'. People may question whether his mother was in fact his father's principal wife. More difficult is the question whether a man is to count as the son of the man who begot him, or as the son of that man's deceased elder brother on behalf of whom this man begot him through the institution of the levirate, the 'raising up of seed' to a man who dies without heirs. Successfully to claim that your genitor was in fact the surrogate of a man much senior to himself can substantially advance you in rank. Of course no one can verify the facts; the acceptance of the claim is the measure of your political weight. If you are sufficiently widely recognized to be the successor of the actual incumbent of a chiefship, he will 'turn out to have been' merely a regent who must make way for you. It is this that led an informant to say to Comaroff (1974: 40): 'Many chiefs are born, and some are robed with the leopard skin, but few die as chiefs.' No doubt this continuance of the contest after the investment of a chief becomes less likely as kingdoms are established and power is concentrated at the centre; and it becomes impossible in practice once the power of the ruler is guaranteed by an external authority. In theory superior rulers are responsive to the dissatisfaction of their subjects' subjects; in practice they incline to support the man to whom they have committed themselves, and when chiefs have been dismissed from office under colonial rule it has usually been for some shortcoming in their role as bureaucrats.

CHAPTER X
CONQUERED KINGS

WHEN a kingdom with any organized hierarchy of authorities is conquered by an outsider, it is rational for the conqueror to maintain this hierarchy in being as the most convenient way of attaining his own ends. The aims of African conquerors were very similar to those of their new subjects; in essence they were to extend the area from which resources and manpower could be obtained. In the main, vassal chiefs ruled their subjects as they had when they were independent. The contrast between Zaria under Sokoto and Zaria under Britain makes the point. The Fulani conquerors altered the rules of succession, the ranking of titled offices and the principles of recruitment to office; but the functions and activities of fief-holders were what their predecessors' had been. The British sought agents for all sorts of policies that had never been heard of before; they demanded the renunciation of lucrative and, before their coming, respectable practices such as slave-raiding and slave-trading, and they sought to establish new principles in such matters as tax-gathering and the administration of justice. It is the uneasy coupling of political systems with divergent aims and principles that gives its interest to the history of kingdoms under colonial rule.

British and French attitudes towards indigenous rulers have often been sharply contrasted, but where they were dealing with kingdoms of substantial proportions the contrast was not as great as might appear at first sight. The French feared that kings would lead rebellions; they deprived them of all but their ritual functions, but they kept the administrative framework of the kingdoms in being. The British deposed those kings whom they conquered but replaced them with men who had a claim to succeed in traditional terms, and they usually maintained the boundaries that they found. They held that law and order depended upon the continuation of traditional authority; that

African ideas of legitimacy would be outraged by the rejection of traditional claims to rule and the substitution for their own kings and chiefs of mere nominees of the new conquerors; that Africans were inherently predisposed towards hereditary rule. The term 'indirect rule', to refer to a system in which subject kingdoms are administered by their own rulers under an over-lord, was first used in the context of Nigeria. It is a cliché nowadays to say that it was an expedient which later become a philosophy, and to ascribe the policy to the fact that in the early days in Nigeria there were very few administrative offi-cers. It would be more accurate to say that the British in nor-thern Nigeria did just what their predecessors had done and what any intelligent person does who takes over a highly organized going concern. Indirect Rule became a philosophy when it was held that *every* African political unit must be administered through its traditional authority, and petty chief-doms of a few thousand population or even village groups with no single head were stretched to fit a Procrustes' bed originally made for the Sultan of Sokoto. Yet it is the fact that people whose chiefs or kings had previously been disregarded were gratified when they were given recognition, and that there has often been dissatisfaction, sometimes even rebellion, when a 'native authority' was appointed who was not considered to have the appropriate qualifications. As Lombard (1967: 104) points out, it was particularly in the early period, when both king and people saw the new ruler as a victorious enemy, that their solidarity was complete. Later, when the co-operation by virtue of which the kings were able to survive began to be seen as a betrayal of their subjects, they became the object of criticism and political opposition.

It was assumed that under European rule African kings would cease to be arbitrary rulers moved only by their 'whims'—as Europeans perceived them—and become ben-evolent monarchs dispensing impartial justice and devoting themselves to the welfare of their subjects. They lost the power of life and death which many had exercised freely both for ritual purposes and to punish disobedience. Their judicial powers were limited, sometimes very narrowly, and their decisions were subject to appeals to European authorities. They were required to replace tribute in kind by regular taxation in cash at fixed rates; though, as before, they passed on a portion of the tax collected to the superior government. Lugard said that a tax must be imposed because it was the traditional symbol of subjection, but of course it had more practical reasons.

More far-reaching in its effect on the position of kings was the endeavour to enlist them on the side of progress in the sense of improved living standards. The people listen to the chief, was the argument; let him be our mouthpiece in persuading them to send their children to school, to contour-ridge their fields, to plant new crops and plant them where and how the agronomists recommend, to dig latrines . . . and so on. The larger the kingdom, the less the king himself could be expected to pass on the message directly to the people; in such a case the advice would be given to his subordinates, but he would be expected to use his influence in the same direction.

In one sense the indirect rule principle worked best in the great kingdoms where it was first introduced. The tax-gathering and judicial organizations were efficient, the revenues were large simply because the populations were large and in Kano, the wealthiest of them, they were expended on impressive modern-style installations, piped water, electricity, a printing-press, a well-equipped hospital, and a number of schools. Critics remarked that expenditure on activities of this kind was concentrated in the capital, but only at a very late date in the colonial period was it found possible to increase the share of tax collected that was to stay at village or district level.

Asante had a peculiar history. After British authority was extended over it in 1896, its separate chiefdoms were treated as independent units, Kumase being merely one among many, and the Asantehene in exile. Only in 1932 was he brought home and restored to his position as head of the Asante Confederacy, as it was now officially named. During the period of interregnum the Gold Coast, as it was then called, depended for central government revenues entirely on customs duties, and the chiefdoms met their internal needs from rents paid by cocoa farmers and, if they were fortunate, mining royalties. They had a new incentive for extending their boundaries, no longer by war but by litigation. As the British saw it, they squandered on these contests money that they raised by *ad hoc* levies on their subjects; on one occasion the government took control of a Stool treasury because it was bankrupt. But it was only in 1936 that all Stool finances were made subject to accounting and supervision; and much later than that Asante chiefs were managing to keep their revenues separate from public funds.

Kings, once recognized by the overlords, had their full political support. Dissent of a kind that would have been possible before—whether or not it was regarded as rebellion—was now treated as subversion. The manpower demands that could be made on subjects, however, were defined, limited, often commuted for a money payment; in British territories there were not complaints that government authorized undue exactions.

The theory that kings and their chiefs, having been persuaded of the desirability of changes in their mode of life, would impose on their people regulations requiring these changes to be made, led to two alternative results; either the 'native authorities' avoided making themselves unpopular by not enforcing the regulations, or they did enforce them and so came to be more and more identified with the alien government. Nowhere did they pass on to their subjects the arguments for innovation, which they very likely did not fully understand themselves. Agricultural regulations often involved harder work than traditional methods required, and their value was not immediately apparent. However, in British territories direct compulsion to labour was not a normal form of exercise of chiefly authority.

In Rwanda the traditional claims of king and chiefs on the labour of their subjects were heavier than anything recorded elsewhere in the Interlacustrine kingdoms (and of course heavier than in those kingdoms where kings and chiefs commanded the labour of slaves). They had required one day's labour in five, but up to 1933, relying on the support of Belgian authority, they increased this to two or three out of six. In that year their claims were commuted for a money payment, but both before and after this date they were required by the Belgians to impose compulsory labour for the cultivation of

cash crops and for re-afforestation and the terracing of slopes
(Lemarchand 1970: 122) and could be punished if they failed
to do so. Here was a specific local reason to add to the dissatisfaction with traditional authority that became vocal in most of
the kingdoms after the second world war.

In French West Africa policy was directed first to the diminution of the authority of kings by removing from their control
populations which had recently been conquered; and also by
deposing or pensioning off such monarchs as the king of
Dahomey and placing other members of the royal family in
charge of divisions of the kingdom. Later the French found that
they could rely for their administrative needs only on 'chiefs
who were listened to'; but they never believed, as did the more
romantic among British thinkers, that the kingdoms could be
modernized and remain a permanent feature of the political
scene. One governor described the role of the Sultan of
Baguirmi as that of an agent of French policy with no right of
independent initiative (Lombard 1967b: 129).

The opposition to kings and chiefs from their own subjects
followed a parallel course in British and French territories. The
general populace may have suffered from abuses of power, but
it was the educated commoners who began to assert claims to
be the true élite in the modern world which their schooling and
experience enabled them to understand. Indeed it was they
who were referred to as the élite by the French authorities.
Profoundly committed as they were to the values of their own
culture, the French emphasized the mastery of their language
in the schools and encouraged the most successful pupils to go
to France for further study. When they came back with
advanced political views, authority was alarmed and fell back
on the argument—which had some substance in this case—that
the young politicians were alienated from the mass of their
people, that the true spokesmen of the masses were the chiefs.
Hence, as late as 1932, French policy turned to reinforcing
chiefly authority, though this hardly went to the length of
restoring deposed kings.

If 1932 was too late to recreate kingship, it was early to be
confronted with political demands. In the British territories
these only began to be heard during the Second World War,

and they took the form of demands for elective institutions to replace those based on heredity before the question of independence began to be mooted. Kings and chiefs were represented as illiterate and out of touch with modern developments, a stereotype which did not conform to the facts, since most of them were literate and many had been in some form of employment before their accession.

The role of chiefs and kings was much debated in the discussions of political evolution which began during the war and continued without interruption until all the British territories were independent. The Aitken Watson Commission, sent to the then Gold Coast after the riots of ex-servicemen in 1948, stated in its report that 'the star of the chiefs has set.' But the locally based Coussey Commission which made the first proposals for constitutional advance was by no means eager to do away with them, and produced a constitution which found a place for chiefs in representative institutions. African politicians favoured the substitution of elected local authorities on the English model for 'native authorities', but with the proviso that kings and chiefs should be ceremonial heads who would open a session and then withdraw. In Ghana, where the revenues of the Stool—not of the individual incumbent—had never been effectively brought to account in native treasuries, chiefs were paid salaries intended to enable them to live in an appropriate style and perform their ritual responsibilities.

Although, in the period of constitution-making before independence, African politicians seemed to be not wholly dedicated to the destruction of royal or chiefly power, the new rulers soon found that they could not tolerate any potential focus of opposition. In English-speaking West Africa kings and chiefs still exist, but they play no formal part in the government of their subjects, let alone that of the nation as a whole. Local administration is in the hands of nominees of a single party or a military government. The great Emirates of northern Nigeria have been broken up, as their neighbours were by the French, into smaller units, each directly responsible to a centrally appointed superior.

The history of the kingdoms in Uganda illustrates the difference between the British attitude to kings and that of independent African leaders. Nowhere, except in Basutoland and Swaziland, did a king's dominions extend to the frontier of a colony which was to become independent. In all the rest of the new states, there were populations which owed no allegiance to a king, and very often the new political leaders were drawn from these. The story of Uganda just before and after independence dramatically illustrates the relations between kings and their own subjects, kings and the British authorities, kings and politicians who were not their subjects. Of the four Uganda kingdoms, Buganda was by far the richest and most populous, though of course its population was a minority in the country as a whole. Many Ganda, looking back to their traditions of conquest, assumed that they would dominate an independent Uganda—just what the peoples of the north feared and resented. In the years before independence the kingship and its incumbent had been criticized from within Buganda, and the king was perceived by some of the politically-minded as a *fainéant* foisted on them by the British. But when a British Governor deposed him because he refused to implement a democratic reform, he became a martyr overnight; and from that time on he was the symbol of his country's prestige. He was restored as a 'constitutional monarch', and as independence approached he and his supporters succeeded in obtaining a large degree of local autonomy for Buganda and a smaller degree of independence from the centre for the other kingdoms. By this time, it is clear, what was at stake was the status of the unit symbolized by the king, not devotion to monarchy as a form of government. The Kabaka of Buganda became President of Uganda, but with narrower powers than most presidents have; there was a moment when he and the elected Prime Minister—Obote, a man from the kingless north—each claimed to have dismissed the other. But the final collapse of kingship was sudden. Obote suspected the Kabaka of plotting a military coup and took the initiative himself; and his army drove all the kings into exile.

Even more dramatic was the end of the kings in Rwanda, which was brought about not by a *coup d'état* but by a popular revolution (tacitly assisted by a Belgian administration which had swung from support of traditional authority to that commitment to the democratization of Africa which Harold Macmillan called 'the wind of change').

Many African kings, then, are living, or have died, in exile. But some are still on their thrones, and one must ask what their status means today. The Hausa kingdoms in the north of Nigeria have been broken up into districts and sub-districts under authorities directly appointed by the military governors of the six states that were created by General Gowon. Through Ghana's history up to the present the Asante kings Prempeh II and his successor Opoku Ware II have remained in office, the former first supported by the British but reduced to the status of an elected local authority, then losing all political recognition when elective bodies were dissolved, the latter the chief custodian of the Asante tradition which is now being so diligently studied by Ghanaian historians.

In Yoruba country the kings are still believed by the general populace to hold the power that was long since taken from them in fact. When during the Nigerian civil war taxes were steeply increased, rioters attacked the palaces of several Obas, and one was killed. But the attempt to introduce elected authorities who would administer welfare services and local amenities has left behind it only a local bureaucracy—still called 'council officials'—who run their districts in colonial style.

Nowadays in Africa there are more dictators than kings.

BIBLIOGRAPHY

ARGYLE, W. J. (1966). *The Fon of Dahomey*, Oxford.

ASHTON, E. H. (1952). *The Basuto*, London.

BALANDIER, G. (1974). *Anthropo-logiques*, Paris.

BARNES, J. A. (1954). *Politics in a Changing Society*, London.

BEATTIE, J. H. M. (1971). *The Nyoro State*, Oxford.

BEIDELMAN, T. O. (1966). 'Swazi Royal Ritual', *Africa*, xxxvi. 373–405.

BLACK-MICHAUD, J. (1975). *Cohesive Force*, Oxford.

BOVILL, E. (1968). *The Golden Trade of the Moors* (2nd edition), Oxford.

BRADBURY, R. E. (1973). *Benin Studies*, Oxford.

COLSON, E. M. (1975). *Tradition and Contract*, London.

COMAROFF, J. L. (1974). 'Chiefship in a South African Homeland', *Journal of Southern African Studies*, 1. 36–51.

CRUICKSHANK, B. (1853). *Eighteen Years on the Gold Coast of Africa*, London (reprinted 1966).

DE HEUSCH, L. (1958). *Essais sur le symbolisme de l'inceste royale*, Brussels.

EVANS-PRITCHARD, E. E. (1940). *The Nuer*, Oxford.

—— (1971). *The Azande*, Oxford.

FALLERS, L. A. ed. (1964). *The King's Men*, London.

GLÉLÉ, M. A. (1974). *Le Danxome*, Paris.

GLUCKMAN, M. ed. (1951). *Seven Tribes of British Central Africa*, London.

—— (1954). *Rituals of Rebellion in South-East Africa*, London.

—— (1963). 'The Rise of a Zulu Empire', *Scientific American*, 202.

GOODY, J. R. ed. (1966). *Succession to High Office*, Cambridge.

—— ed. (1968). *Literacy in Traditional Societies*, Cambridge.

GORJU, J. (1920). *Entre le Victoria, l'Albert et l'Edouard*, Marseilles.

JINGOES, S. J. (1975). *A Chief is a Chief by the People*, London.

'K. W.' (1937). 'The procedure in accession to the throne of a nominated King in the kingdom of Bunyoro', *Uganda Journal*, 4.

KARUGIRE, S. R. (1971). *A History of the Kingdom of Nkore in Western Uganda*, Oxford.

KUPER, H. (1947). *An African Aristocracy*, London.

LABAT, J. B. (1730). *Voyage du chevalier Des Marchais en Guinée, isles voisines, et en Cayenne, fait in 1725, 1726 et 1727*, vol. 2, Paris.

LEMARCHAND, R. (1970). *Rwanda and Burundi*, London.

LLOYD, P. C. (1960). 'Sacred Kingship and Government among the Yoruba', *Africa*, xxx. 221–37.

—— (1971). *The Political Development of Yoruba Kingdoms in the Eighteenth and Nineteenth Centuries*, London.

LOMBARD, J. A. (1965). *Structures de type 'féodal' en Afrique Noire*, Paris.

—— (1967a). 'The Kingdom of Dahomey', in Forde D. and Kaberry, P. M., eds., *West African Kingdoms in the Nineteenth Century*, London.

—— (1967b). *Autorités Traditionelles et Pouvoirs Européens en Afrique Noire*, Paris.

MAQUET, J. J. (1961). *The Premise of Inequality in Ruanda*, London.

MAYER, P. (1949). *The Lineage Principle in Gusii Society*, London.

MERCIER, P. (1954). 'The Fon of Dahomey', in Forde D., ed., *African Worlds*, London.

MORTON-WILLIAMS, P. (1960). 'The Yoruba Ogboni Cult in Oyo', *Africa*, xxx, 362–74.

—— (1967). 'The Yoruba Kingdom of Oyo', in Forde, D. and Kaberry, P., eds., *West African Kingdoms in the Nineteenth Century*, London.

MUDANDAGIZI, V. (with Rwamukumbi, J.) (1974). 'Les formes historiques de la dépendence personnelle dans l'État rwandais', *Cahiers d'Études Africaines*, 6. 26–53.

NEWBURY, C. (1961). *The Western Slave Coast and its Neighbours*, London.

NADEL, S. F. (1942). *A Black Byzantium*, London.

OBERG, K. (1940). 'The Kingdom of Ankole in Uganda', in Evans-Pritchard, E. E. and Fortes, M. eds., *African Political Systems*, London.

OLIVER, R. and FAGE, J. D. (1962). *A Short History of Africa*, Harmondsworth.

OMER-COOPER, J. B. (1966). *The Zulu Aftermath*, London.

RATTRAY, R. S. (1923). *Ashanti*, Oxford.

—— (1929). *Ashanti Law and Constitution*, Oxford.

READ, M. (1956). *The Ngoni of Nyasaland*, London.

REINDORF, C. C. (1895). *History of the Gold Coast*, Basel (reprinted London, 1966).

RUEL, M. (1969). *Leopards and Leaders*, London.

RWAMUKUMBA, J. (with Mudandagizi, V.) (1974). 'Les formes historiques de la dépendence personnelle dans l'État rwandais', *Cahiers d'Études Africaines*, 6. 26–53.

SANSOM, B. (1974). 'Traditional Economic Systems', in Hammond-Tooke, W. D., ed., *The Bantu-Speaking Peoples of Southern Africa*, London.

SKERTCHLY, J. (1874). *Dahomey as it is*, London.

SMITH, M. G. (1960). *Government in Zazzau*, London.

SOUTHWOLD, M., n.d. (1961). *Bureaucracy and Chiefship in Buganda*, London.

THOMPSON, L. (1969). 'The Zulu Kingdom in Natal', in Wilson, M. and Thompson, L., eds., *Oxford History of South Africa*, Oxford.

TURNER, V. W. (1969). *The Ritual Process*, London.

URVOY, Y. (1936). *Histoire des populations du Soudan central*, Paris.

VANSINA, J. (1962). *L'évolution du royaume rwanda des origines à 1900*, Brussels.

—— (1966). *Kingdoms of the Savanna*, Madison, Wisconsin.

WILKS, L. (1975). *Asante in the Nineteenth Century*, Cambridge.

WILSON, G. (1939). *The Constitution of Ngonde*, Livingstone.

WILSON, M. (1959). *Communal Rituals of the Nyakyusa*, London.

INDEX